Consulted to Death

CONSULTED TO DEATH

DOUG SMITH

ARBEITER RING PUBLISHING • WINNIPEG

Copyright ©2010 Doug Smith

Arbeiter Ring Publishing
201E-121 Osborne Street
Winnipeg, Manitoba
Canada R3L 1Y4
www.arbeiterring.com

Printed in Canada by Imprimerie Gauvin
Cover by Doowah Design
Seventh Printing, 2012

With assistance of the Manitoba Arts Council/Conseil des Arts du Manitoba, the
Boag Foundation, the Douglas-Coldwell Foundation, the Canadian Union of Public
Employees-Manitoba, the Manitoba Government Employees' Union, and the Joseph
Zuken Memorial Foundation.

We acknowledge the support of the Canada Council for our publishing program.

ARP acknowledges the financial support to our publishing activities of the Manitoba
Arts Council/Conseil des Arts du Manitoba, Manitoba Culture, Heritage and Tourism,
and the Government of Canada through the Canada Book Fund.

Arbeiter Ring Publishing acknowledges the support of the Province of Manitoba through
the Book Publishing Tax Credit and the Book Publisher Marketing Assistance Program.

LIBRARY AND ARCHIVES CANADA CATALOGUING IN PUBLICATION

Smith, Doug, 1954–
    Consulted to death: how Canada's workplace health and safety system
fails workers

ISBN 1-894037-08-1

    1. Industrial hygene--Canada. 2. Industrial safety--Canada.
3. Workers' compensation--Canada. i. Title.

HD7658.S48 2000   363'110971   C00-920220-X

to Judy Cook,
gentle comrade

ACKNOWLEDGEMENTS & ATTRIBUTIONS

THIS WORK DRAWS ON TWENTY years of journalism. The prospect of drawing up a list of all the people to whom I have incurred a debt of gratitude during that period is intimidating. I must start by thanking all the workers who agreed to speak with me about their jobs and their health over the past two decades. It is to you that I owe my greatest debts.

Over the years I have spoken with many people about this topic and been commissioned to engage in a variety of research projects in this area. What follows is my best effort at acknowledging my teachers and my benefactors. I suspect that some people will wonder why their names are on this list, but at some point or other they helped. Thanks to Jay Cowan, Luis Rufo, Victor Rabinovith, Richard Starr, Kris Klaasen, Skip Hambling, Judy Cook, Bev Cann, Dorothy Wigmore, Lisa Donner, Dr. Allen Kraut, Dr. Annalee Yassi, Dr. Ahmod Randeree, Diane Gagnon, Lynn Bueckert (in fact, the whole staff of the MFL Occupational Health Centre, past and present), Ivan Sabesky, Gerry Adolphe, Dick Martin, Pat Martin, Linda Boles, Mike MacIsaac, Harry Mesman, Peter Walker, Bob Sass, Wayne Roberts, Margaret Ingram, Eric Tucker, Jim Brophy, Margaret Keith, Margaret Day, Bob Sample, Doug Sprague, Gerry Friesen, Joel Novek, and Nolan Reilly. I know that names have been left off—I am sorry.

Bill Blaikie and Allen Seager were instrumental in providing funding for this project.

Thanks to the editors past and present of *The Last Post*, *This Magazine*, *Canadian Dimension*, *Canadian Forum*, the *Inner City Voice*, *The Voice*, and the *Winnipeg Sun*, who have published some of the work on which this book is based. Furthermore, I would like to thank the various CBC producers I worked with on occupational health and safety stories.

Todd Scarth and John Samson of Arbeiter Ring were enthusiastic supporters of this project from the outset. They, along with Esyllt Jones and Ria Julien, have made sure that my dealings with the press have been as painless as possible.

Steven Rosenberg, Terry Gallagher, Rob Niedzwiecki, and the rest of the staff at Doowah Design: if only I could write a book worthy of being judged by your covers.

Family can still be a haven in a heartless world, and I speak from blessed experience: thank you, Sandra and Erica.

Attributions

As noted above, I have been writing and researching this topic for twenty years. I have footnoted most of the quotations and information in this book. I have not, however, footnoted my own interviews or my own journalism. I realize this violates the first rule of the academy, namely, "If I do not cite myself, who will?" but so be it.

CONTENTS

INTRODUCTION

IT WAS ONLY ON THE SPUR OF the moment that Jim Brophy, Bob McArthur and a group of other young Windsor, Ontario workers drove down to Toronto to attend the Ontario Federation of Labour's 1981 workplace health and safety conference. Brophy, an American expatriate and refugee from the Chrysler engine plant, had spent the last few years working on behalf of autoworkers who were dying from on-the-job exposure to asbestos. McArthur was a salt-miner—building cars wasn't the only dirty and dangerous job in Windsor—and a health and safety activist in his union. They were doubtful that there was much that a bunch of labour leaders could tell them about on-the-job issues. Nor did the agenda look all that promising. The keynote speaker was the assistant deputy minister of labour from Saskatchewan. But just before they left Windsor, someone had the good sense to take along a cheap cassette tape recorder.

The first thought that passed through their minds when Bob Sass, the government official from Saskatchewan, got up to give his after-dinner speech was, "this guy's not from Saskatchewan." A native of New York, Sass spoke with the inflections of the Lower East Side. And the second thought was, "this guy can't be from the government." Here was a bureaucrat who was telling them not to trust government, not to trust the employer, to trust only their own knowledge and experience. Sass joked about what he called the village idiot theory that blamed careless workers for accidents, pointing out that this widely held management belief rested on no scientific research. He said professionals were not disinterested experts, but often well-paid hired guns who defended corporate interests. The group from Windsor knew that—probably everyone at the conference suspected as much—but they never expected to hear it from a government official. Breathing fire, Sass was preaching the hot gospel of workplace health and safety. His speech built in intensity as he worked toward his conclusion: that work could only be made safer when workers had a real say in how things were done. It climaxed with one of Sass's most famous and repeated formulations.

> There has been a lot discussion in the last days here about how information is power. We need the right to know, we need information. But remember: power is power.

The audience went wild. Small wonder the Windsor workers were sitting around over their late night drinks asking themselves, "who was that masked man?" Today Brophy is the director of the Windsor branch of the Occupational Clinic for Ontario Workers. He still talks about the speech and its impact. "It confirmed all the things that we had been thinking but had not been able to articulate or put into such a powerful framework."

You can still hear the speech. Brophy had no problem digging up a copy for me when I interviewed him in the fall of 1998. In the early 1980s the tape was the workplace health and safety equivalent of the Great White Wonder, the mythic bootleg recording of Bob Dylan live at Albert Hall. Or, perhaps, the Canadian equivalent of a Lech Walesa speech in Poland. Brophy recalls,

> We were reading a lot about *Solidarnosc* in Poland and how workers were circulating audio tapes and books in the underground and how they were being passed from hand to hand. And that is what happened to Bob Sass's tape. It just went all over the place. All the activists wanted copies to play for people. To say "This is what it is that we are talking about. This sense that this experience in the workplace and how our health is affected by it is really a way of looking at society and our role in it and really what our problems are."

In the 1970s and 1980s Bob Sass was the Billy Sunday of Canada's occupational health and safety movement. No provincial federation of labour health and safety conference was complete without his presence. Cathy Walker, who today is the health and safety director for the Canadian Autoworkers, recalls her first exposure to Sass. "He was really a firebrand and a very inspiring person. At conferences, seminars, meetings, rallies, wherever he came to speak, people just caught the health and safety bug and decided they were going to go out and change their workplace and save the world."

Sass did more than tell workers what was wrong. Like any good evangelical, Bob was preaching salvation through the trinity, although it was a decidedly secular trinity. He was a champion of what became known as the three Rs. Workers had to have the right to know what they were working with, the right to participate in decisions affecting their health, and the right to refuse work that they believed to be dangerous. Sass's three Rs were a departure from the century-old approach that held that workers and management had identical interests when it came to health and safety, and so the issue could simply be left in management's hands. They were also a departure from the traditional trade-union demand for tougher health and safety laws and better inspection. Workers could not put their faith in the boss or the government, Sass said. They had to save themselves. And the three Rs would provide them with the power to do so.

I was a Bob Sass convert. He got me in the spring of 1980, when he spoke at a conference on health and safety at the University of Manitoba. Listening to the tinny, distorted cassette recording from twenty years ago I remember why. Sass's passion and energy rip through the static, the distortion and the years, taking me back to a time when there was a vibrant and exciting health and safety movement in this country.

In the late 1970s in Manitoba, Luis Rufo, a tool-and-die maker turned Moulders Union representative, attacked the Conservative government over the issue of industrial lead poisoning. Company doctors had kept workers in the dark about their health conditions and the risks they faced. The provincial director of workplace health and safety resigned in protest saying the government was sitting on damning evidence of what amounted to an epidemic of lead poisoning. Jay Cowan, the New Democratic Party's labour critic and a former miner, was uncovering a different set of betrayed and poisoned workers every day.

While it was clear that, as the title of one of the handbooks of that era had it, work is dangerous to your health, it was very heaven to be a young left-wing journalist at that time. I wrote a booklet for Rufo on lead poisoning, produced a documentary series on health and safety for the CBC (and along the way interviewed Bob Sass for the first time), wrote pamphlets for the local federation of labour's health and safety committee, and helped make a fundraising slide-tape show— does anyone still know what a slide-tape show is?—for a worker-run health clinic.

But along the way, for a variety of reasons, the volume got turned down. First, the health and safety movement won a lot of battles. Governments across Canada incorporated the three Rs into their health and safety laws. Tens of thousands of workers took health and safety training, joint health-and-safety committees sprang up in workplaces across the country. Now it was up to the workers to save themselves. But workers were in an uphill struggle. Two punishing recessions took a lot of the jam out the Canadian labour movement in the 1980s and the 1990s. Everyone feared that if they pushed the boss too hard, he might go out of business or, as free trade agreements came into effect, to Mexico. Many workers chose to eat smoke at work so they could put food on the table at home.

I kept my hand in, doing the odd health and safety story as I pursued a career as a freelance writer and broadcaster. From the late 1980s onwards I edited a newsletter for the Manitoba Federation of Labour's Occupational Health Centre. And every now and then I would wonder, just how effective were the reforms of the 1970s? From interviews I had done with workers over the years, I realized that few people had experienced these rights as the liberation that we had hoped for. In 1998 I convinced the CBC Radio program *Ideas* to let me try to answer my question. I would like to say that I spoke with academics and workers from across the country, but CBC budgets are not so expansive. Instead I took a trip though Ontario's industrial heartland: Hamilton, Windsor, Sarnia. ("With that itinerary," a perceptive friend said, "you've got to be working on a labour story.") I spent a day with Bob Sass at his home in Saskatoon. And I spoke with Manitoba workers whose stories I had been reporting on for two decades. The resulting program, "Health for Sale," was broadcast in September 1999.

This book is an expansion of that program. It is not an overview of current health and safety risks in Canada, or even of current laws. Nor does it survey the risks that workers face. Instead it is an exploration of how some workers experienced a set of reforms that were meant to both democratize the workplace and make it safer and healthier. That this book draws a critical conclusion should not been seen as a judgement on the last generation of activists and reformers, or the work that current health and safety committee members are doing. There have been times when, as I listened to a worker tell me how the new health and safety committee had been unable to wring any meaningful changes from management, I felt a twinge of shame for having once helped tout this system. But then I recall one such worker's parting comments on the doorstep, made, typically, after the tape recorder had been turned off and packed away. "Yeah," he said, "the laws don't do very much. But you know, if they weren't there, the employer would be doing even less."

1

HEALTH FOR SALE

IN THE SUMMER OF 1991 BILL QUINN and his wife Hannelore were carrying a chair out the basement of their home in the Winnipeg suburb of Transcona. Quinn felt himself growing short of breath. Like generations of men from Transcona, Quinn worked in the Canadian National Railways' Symington Yards, located just a few blocks away from the Quinn's well-maintained bungalow. A pipefitter by training, he was aware of the dangers of working on the railway. But it was in the safety of his home, on his basement steps, not in the noisy, dusty yards, that he felt the burden of years of railway work. "I fell down, I got up. We tried to take it further. I got about three steps and that was it. I could not do anything."

Quinn was taken to hospital. There he was diagnosed as suffering from interstitial lung disease—a scarring of the lungs. It was the start of a legal and medical battle that would last until Quinn's death in 1996. Before he died, Quinn underwent a lung transplant and a successful struggle with the Manitoba Workers' Compensation Board to win benefits for himself and his family.

Quinn started working at the Symington Yards in 1974. I interviewed him twenty years later, for an article I was writing for the Manitoba Federation of Labour Occupational Health Centre newsletter. He told me, "I gave them the best years of my life. I worked on every kind of dangerous situation. I worked with asbestos and silica sand, and around PCBs and other dangerous products." As he described it, the CN wash pit—where he spent much of his career—

was dirty, smoky, and dangerous. Often it was so smoky, it was impossible to see from one side of the pit to the other. There are hundreds of miles of pipe on a diesel engine. A railway pipefitter spends much of his time cleaning and mending those pipes. Pipefitters weld, burnish, and use powerful cleaners and solvents. The extreme temperatures and high-powered hoses release dozens of chemicals into the air.

> "We used to work with raw asbestos and mix it up into pipe covering. We would use certain parts of asbestos and lime and cement and we would mix it all together. We would also strip asbestos off cars without respirators on. Nobody said it was dangerous to do. When we were finished working with asbestos, without any respirators on or anything, we would blow our clothes off and all the particles would become airborne and we would pollute the whole shop."

Quinn said that he often raised concerns about the dangers of airborne substances in the workplace, but management contended there was adequate ventilation. For many years, he said, the company's only safety concern was whether workers had their steel-toed boots on or not.

Once Quinn—who was a non-smoker—was in the hospital, his family turned to the task of trying to win him workers' compensation. This was not easy, because the system is stacked against workers who are claiming compensation for an industrial disease. A worker who is injured by a fall from a ladder has relatively little problem winning a workers' compensation claim. But it is far more difficult to prove that one's illness was caused by one's job. Quinn was fortunate in that his union made arrangements to have Len Wheeler, a fellow CN employee, take on his case. Wheeler had spent much of the previous ten years honing his skills as a workers' compensation advocate. When he realized that this was an industrial disease case, he told Quinn that he could expect a long battle. Quinn did not feel up to pursuing the case, but Wheeler convinced him not to give up. The first step was to have Dr. Allen Kraut of the Manitoba Federation of Labour Occupational Health Centre examine Quinn.

Kraut visited Quinn in the hospital and inspected his work site. There was no obvious cause of the disease, but there were numerous substances in the workplace that could have contributed to Quinn's condition. Kraut had a sample of Quinn's lung sent to a laboratory in the United States where it was subjected to a type of test known as ashing. The lung tissue was burned and examined for metal particles. It revealed very high levels of such metals as aluminum, copper, titanium, iron, chromium, tin, manganese, barium, cerium, and zinc. When Kraut reviewed the medical literature on interstitial lung disease, he uncovered a British study that concluded that metal workers who had no other obvious cause for the disease were ten times more likely than the average person to develop it.

At the same time, Wheeler reviewed all the data sheets that CN has to make available on the products to which employees are exposed. He discovered that all the metals the ashing test had found in Quinn's lungs had also been present in this workplace. Still, the Manitoba Workers' Compensation Board twice rejected his claim. Wheeler, who Quinn referred to as his "lifesaver," prepared a four-and-a-half hour presentation to the Compensation Board's Appeal Commission. In it, he linked his research with Kraut's findings and the results of the ashing test. The commission granted Quinn his benefits in 1994. As Quinn put it, "the CNR made me sick and we proved it."

Like many workers, Bill Quinn knew his workplace was dangerous. And he wanted to see it cleaned up. He was an active member of the joint workplace health and safety committee in the plant. He said he was constantly raising concerns about his work area. "Every day I work in the area and I feel it is hurting me. I said, 'One of these days somebody is going to get hurt. It is going to be bad.' Not knowing that I was the one getting hurt and not knowing I was the one who was going to get a lung transplant."

Nor was he impressed with CN's approach to workplace health and safety education. Often the educational sessions involved little more than having one worker reading aloud from a safety manual to the other workers. "That's not the CN teaching the men, that's the men teaching the men." Which might not necessarily be so bad, but in these cases workers would simply be "stumbling along in some book they knew nothing about."

At the time we spoke, CN was considering appealing the WCB ruling to the courts. Quinn said he was sick with anxiety. He still had only 30 percent of his original lung capacity and he was worried that his body might reject his new lungs.

After I turned off my tape recorder, we continued to chat. As always, the conversation flows freest in these situations. Quinn expressed his gratitude to Len Wheeler and his bitterness toward the company and the way its health and safety programs had failed. I turned the machine back on and had him retell one anecdote about his conflicts with the railway about job-site inspections. According to Quinn these were always conducted under ideal conditions. Completely different—and safer—work practices were used on test days. "And," said an exasperated Quinn, "they had the windows open. So that everything was vented outside, plus out their antiquated little exhaust system."

Quinn recalled how during one of these inspections, he raised all these issues with the official who was doing the testing. "He would not listen to me. And one of the other guys that worked with me came up and was listening to me talking to him. My friend said, 'Could I see your clipboard for a minute.' He said, 'Okay.' And the worker took the clipboard and banged the inspector on the head with the clipboard saying, 'You are obviously not listening to what he is telling you. That is what is happening in this area—you are not testing under the right conditions and we all know that.'" When the inspector threatened to report the worker, Quinn said he told the inspector, "I am not going to be a witness to that. I never saw anything."

Afterwards, Quinn continued to argue that the tests had been improperly conducted. "And the CNR would argue that the test was done. And the test, it said it was okay. That is the CNR and the wash pit area and the health and safety committee. It is really great."

Bill Quinn's story is unusual. But it is far from unique. He was killed by a disease that he contracted at work. And the health and safety system, which had been established by the Canadian government in the 1970s, failed to protect his health. He was a worker who wanted to be healthy. He did not smoke. He participated in the health and safety committee. He learned about the dangers he was exposed to on the job. He tried to make the system work for him.

And he is far from alone. Allen Kraut has done one of the most comprehensive studies on the extent of occupational disease in Canada. He estimates that between 2,300 and 6,000 Canadians die from occupational disease every year. But many of those workers do not know that their illnesses are caused by their jobs. Without access to a tenacious advocate such as Wheeler, and a physician trained in occupational disease such as Kraut, there is little chance the occupational nature of their illness will be diagnosed and virtually no chance that they will be granted compensation.

On average, one Canadian worker out of fifteen was injured at work in 1996; this is one occupational injury every 9.2 seconds of time worked. One worker out of thirty-two was injured severely enough to miss at least one day of work. This figure represents one time-loss injury every nineteen seconds worked. In Canada, over the period 1970 to 1996, an average of slightly less than one million occupational injuries has been reported each year by provincial or territorial workers' compensation boards (WCBs). Between 1970 and 1996, time-loss injuries were an increasing portion of the occupational injuries, rising from 38 percent in 1970 to a peak of 60 percent in 1987 and declining steadily since then to reach 48 percent in 1996. In 1996, there were 785,666 occupational injuries reported by WCBs. This total included 668 fatalities and 379,554 time-loss injuries compensated by the WCBs.

Carnage in the workplace is a national disgrace. Twenty-five years ago governments across Canada responded to this disgrace by adopting health and safety legislation that aimed to provide workers with more rights in the workplace. The right to refuse dangerous work, the right to participate in health and safety committees, and the right to know about the products they were working with were meant to give workers some ability to protect their health. Few would deny that these were important gains for workers. However, they have not delivered the goods.

Bill Quinn had the right to participate in a health and safety committee. For the most part, these committee meetings did not end with managers getting hit on the head with clipboards, but with committees putting the seal of approval on a workplace that was poisoning Bill's lungs. He had the right to know which products he was working with—in the end this information was most useful to him when he was fighting his claim for compensation. And the right to refuse work was a tough right to exercise during the 1980s when CN was laying off workers at a record pace. There would always be someone willing to breathe a little more dust and smoke if it meant a steady job.

As Bob Sass, the man who helped develop these rights, has sadly concluded, they are weak rights, not strong rights. They have failed because they have not addressed the power relationship at work. As a result, changes meant to empower workers have been used by neoconservative governments to abandon workers and their health to the mercy of the marketplace. In many ways it represents a return to laissez-faire world of the nineteenth century.

WHEN THE INDUSTRIAL REVOLUTION hit Canada in the mid-nineteenth century, there were no health and safety laws. The few existing laws that governed workplaces were often called Master and Servant Acts—and it was very clear who was the master and who was the servant. As late as 1894 the Manitoba government adopted a Master and Servant Act that made it illegal for a "clerk, journeyman, apprentice, servant or laborer" to disobey his or her master. Workers who deserted or abandoned their employer faced a $20 fine or a month in jail.

Workers who were injured on the job had to turn to the courts for assistance. There they could sue their employer for negligence. This process was expensive and chancy. Few injured workers could afford a lawyer, and anyone who was only partially injured knew they were forfeiting any chance of getting their old position back if they sued the boss. Once they were in court they found that the rules were stacked against them.

British and American courts had developed a series of rules that were rigidly applied by Canadian judges. These rules—called the law of employer liability—made it almost impossible for an injured worker to successfully sue her employer.

Under the rule of contributory negligence, the courts refused to award damages if the worker had contributed to the cause of the injury. The second rule held that the employer could not be held responsible if the injury had been caused by the actions of another worker. These two rules effectively blocked many workers from receiving compensation.

But any cases that made it past these two rules were usually stopped by the third, known as the assumption of risk. This rule stated that when a worker took a job he or she was agreeing to assume any risks that were associated with that job. The worker's regular paycheque was compensation in advance for the risks. Once a worker had agreed to run a risk for a certain fee, the judges said it was improper for the courts to step in and make the employer pay additional compensation. That would be interfering with the contract that the worker and employer had freely entered into. Elaborate arguments were made about how these three rules worked together to make workplaces safer. Because workers could not collect benefits if they were at fault, they would be more careful. Since they could not collect if a co-worker was at fault, workers had an incentive to make sure that their co-workers did everything by the book. The principle failing with these arguments is that they were being made at a time when workers were losing control over how they and their co-workers performed their tasks. They were required to work ten- and twelve-hour days with equipment over which they had no control and to meet set production goals if they wanted a living wage.

Judges also argued that the assumption of risk rule served to make workplaces safer. If worker health and safety was for sale in the marketplace, employers would find that they would have to raise wages to high levels before they could find workers to do truly dangerous work. Rather than pay these wages, the employer would make the job safer. It was an elegant argument, but it paid no mind to the fact that in a world of high unemployment and no social security, the choice most workers faced was between working or starving.

In Manitoba the railways made vigorous use of these defenses. In 1888, the family of Nelson Rajotte, a Canadian Pacific Railway switchman who was crushed to death by a train when his foot was caught in the tracks, sued the CPR. When a jury found the railway guilty of negligence, the corporation appealed. It won a new trial, based on the argument that Rajotte had assumed the risk of getting his foot caught when he agreed to work as a switchman. The Manitoba appeal court judge wrote:

> The danger was an open and palpable one. The deceased had quite as good an opportunity of seeing and knowing the danger as the defendants. And where both parties have equal means of knowledge, it has been said the master is under no obligation to provide for the safety of the servant to a greater extent than the servant is bound to provide for his own safety.[1]

When in 1908 a CPR brakeman named Street had one arm and part of a foot cut off after his foot became caught in the railway's Morden yards, he sued for negligence. His lawyer pointed out that, in violation of the Railway Act, the CPR had failed to pack the track to prevent this sort of injury. A jury decided the case in Street's favour and awarded him $10,000. The CPR appealed and the Court of Appeal ruled that the jury had not given sufficient consideration to the railway's argument that the brakeman, in going about his normal duties, had contributed to the injury.[2]

The idea that the relative danger of work was reflected in the wages that people were offered was deeply ingrained. When the Manitoba government overhauled its workers' compensation system in 1916, a Manitoba farmer wrote the government to protest the need for compulsory insurance. He argued, "In operating a threshing machine if a man is running an engine or separator he is paid for the risk he is taking at the rate of from six to ten dollars per day, that wage should be protection enough, a pitcher [of hay] receives from three to three fifty per day and runs practically no risk."[3] But this attitude was coming under attack from the labour movement during the early part of the twentieth century. As an editorial in the Winnipeg *Voice*, the movement's weekly newspaper, noted:

The past week has been more than usually prolific of accidents, resulting in the maiming or killing of wage earners while at their work. Fallings, crushing, cutting, strainings and breakings, the victims have followed one another into the hospitals in close procession in the cities and towns of the west. This fearful tribute which labour pays to capital is almost completely overlooked in the reckoning between them. We are producing spoils, culls, and derelicts at a rapid gait in the west, but the supply of labour is always sufficient to easily fill up the vacancies and all goes on as before.[4]

In light of this, the common view that the marketplace should govern workplace health and safety could not last. It was becoming clear that the public believed employers had to be held responsible for what went on in their workplaces. Jury decisions provide some evidence of popular dissatisfaction with the employer liability defences, since the Court of Appeal was often setting aside decisions and reducing awards in cases where juries had ignored the liability rules and sided with the injured worker.

In 1894 the Manitoba legislature adopted the Workmen's Compensation for Injury Act. Modeled on the British Employers' Liability Act of 1880, it restricted the use employers could make of the three common law defences. Employers were now responsible for the negligence of their employees and were liable for injuries caused by defects in the "ways, works, machinery, or plant connected with, or used in the employer's business."[5] The law still had a number of limitations, perhaps the most significant being the requirement that the injured worker, or the worker's survivors, hire a lawyer and pursue the case in the civil courts. The injured worker also had to prove negligence—if the injury occurred as a part of the "normal" run of affairs, there was no compensation. Workers were not eligible for compensation if they were aware of any defects or negligence and failed to report them in a reasonable period of time. The government was not taking any responsibility for seeing that all injured workers were properly compensated. The compensation awarded under this act could not exceed three years' income. Under the old system victories may have been harder to win, but there was no cap on the size of awards that could be made.

In Manitoba, there were at least eleven cases of the railways appealing decisions made against them prior to 1916. Even when the judges ruled in favour of the injured workers, they often significantly reduced the size of the award. After a jury awarded $7,000 to a CPR employee who had been left blind and deaf after trying, without any training, to thaw dynamite, the appeal court substituted an award of $1,200.[6] In 1909 one alarmed appeal court judge said:

> The tendency of juries to give damages to plaintiffs in such cases is so great that I can not but think that they are frequently influenced to do so by sympathy irrespective of the evidence or the weight of evidence. The practical result of trying such cases by jury is to make employers insurers of their employees' safety, a liability which the law of master and servant does not impose.[7]

Appeal court judges were also likely to define negligence in a more limited manner than a jury would. When the family of a Grand Trunk Pacific Railway employee, who was crushed to death between two cars, sued for negligence, a jury ruled in their favour. However, the court of appeal ruled that since the defect that led to the accident was not visible to "customary inspection," there was no negligence and the case against the railway was dismissed.[8]

Limiting the fearful tribute that labour paid to capital in blood and broken bones was a core demand of the labour movement that was being called into being by the Industrial Revolution. Since the less time you spent at work the safer you were, it can be argued that the Nine Hours League, Canada's first national labour organization, had put health and safety issues at the head of its agenda. In many provinces it was the protracted struggle to reform the workers' compensation laws that turned a collection of local unions and labour councils into a provincial labour movement. These efforts eventually bore fruit. In the first two decades of the last century provincial governments enacted factory acts, requiring employers to meet certain standards and maintain safe workplaces.

The laws were often adopted in response to workplace disasters that had in some way captured the public imagination. In Manitoba, the trigger was the death of Gudrun Johansson, a woman who worked at the Great West Laundry Company. In 1900 Johansson stepped over an unprotected revolving shaft a few inches above the floor and was caught by her skirts. She was "thrown with violence to the floor and so wounded and injured that she died on the same day."[9] In the wake of a public outcry, the Crown brought manslaughter charges against Great West Laundry, claiming the company had maintained "machinery in a condition dangerous to life, resulting in the death of one of its employees." The charges, however, were dropped following an appeal court ruling that "a corporation cannot be indicted for such a crime as manslaughter."[10] Capitalizing on outraged public opinion, unions pressured the Conservative government to pass the province's first Factories Act.[11] The bulk of the act dealt with the employment of women and children. No one under the age of sixteen was to be employed in a factory, and women and young girls could not be employed in a factory for more than forty-eight hours a week—unless an exemption were granted, in which case the work week could reach sixty hours.

In health and safety, the law is important, but enforcement is paramount. It was four years before the Manitoba government appointed a factories inspector—and sixteen years before the job was paid on a full-time basis.[12] In 1910, when the inspector reported that he had made 1,073 inspections that year, the Winnipeg Trades and Labour Council commented that they must have been made "from the outside."[13] Similar stories can be told about factory inspection in every province in Canada.

In 1914 Ontario adopted the first modern workers' compensation system in Canada. Based on a series of recommendations by Ontario Chief Justice Sir William Meredith, the system provided guaranteed benefits on a no-fault basis. Employers would pay into a compensation fund that would be administered by a non-profit agency whose directors were appointed by government, business and labour. Workers' compensation was a mixed blessing. The benefits were a percentage of the injured worker's wages—and were often less than the worker might have won in a successful court case. However, the worker no longer had to sue—and win—to receive benefits. In fact, workers were no longer allowed to sue for negligence if they were covered by the Workmen's Compensation Act.

With the passage of factory acts and the development of the workers' compensation system, workplace health and safety had supposedly passed from the era of market regulation. The state sought to control health and safety by adopting health and safety regulations that employers would have to live up to. At the same time, the new compensation system was forcing employers to assume the cost of on-the-job injuries. In North America this regime was to last until the 1970s.

All of this may read like a history of how workers failed to protect their health and safety. And there were many shortcomings to the compensation and factory act systems. Before reviewing them, it is important to emphasize that this system, which was all that government was prepared to give workers, did make a real difference. It put more money than ever before into the hands of injured workers and their families. As companies saw their workers' compensation premiums climb, they began to invest more money in workplace safety. And there is no denying that these investments brought down the accident rates across industries. Of course, had compensation rates been even higher than the miserly rates that were initially paid, even more money would have gone to injured workers and their families, and employers would have made their workplaces even safer. But this should not obscure the fact that these reforms did improve the lives of working people.

The new health and safety regime operated on the basis of two very important assumptions. The first was that worker carelessness was one of the prime causes of most injuries. The second was that injuries are an unavoidable consequence of industrial production. Employers had won an important if largely unnoticed victory when everyone involved in health and safety began referring to the injuring of a worker as an accident, meaning an unintentional event. From these assumptions there followed a belief that employers and workers had identical interests when it came to health and safety. Therefore, health and safety should be removed from the conflict-ridden world of industrial relations. In reality, it meant that health and safety was left to the employer. Very few workers or unions were allowed to participate in the national and international workplace safety bodies that were established in the early 1920s. After all, there was no need for worker involvement if workers and employers were seen to have the same interests, particularly if worker carelessness was the main cause of most injuries.

Perhaps this system's greatest failing came in the area of occupational health. For while workplaces became safer during the twentieth century, they did not necessarily become healthier. Workplace safety programs seek to eliminate sudden, on-the-job injuries. Safety programs involved putting guards on dangerous equipment and developing safer work processes. Since an injured worker could receive compensation and since production usually shut down following a workplace injury, employers had an incentive to make their workplaces safer. However, there was little incentive to do anything about industrial diseases. Such diseases are brought on by exposure to dangerous substances in the workplace or by the work process itself. Usually they take years to develop. In the case of occupational cancers, the worker may not be diagnosed with cancer until after he or she has left the workforce. Compensation boards only recognized a few occupational diseases and granted compensation to very few workers.

Of course, there was little reason for employers to take action against occupational diseases. There were few or no workers' compensation costs attached to such diseases, they did not disrupt production, and solutions were often very expensive—eliminating lead poisoning, for example, might involve installing a new ventilation system, an investment that might do little to improve productivity.

By the 1960s it was clear to many workers and trade unionists that the approach that had been used up to this point had exhausted its effectiveness. Workplace health and safety inspectors were few and far between, and they were generally proud to state that they only prosecuted employers as a last resort. While there were factory acts and government regulations, employers were, for the most part, free to set their own health and safety regulations. And they opted for only as much safety as they could afford. In other words, workers' health and safety was still a captive of the marketplace. It was in the face of this system that a new workers' health and safety movement emerged in North American in the 1960s and 1970s. It was in response to this movement that governments would adopt new health and safety laws to provide workers with health and safety rights on the job.

2

THE HEALTH AND SAFETY MOVEMENT AND THE COMING OF THE THREE RS

IT SEEMED TO COLIN LAMBERT that there was no way to get management to repair the floor on the powerful drilling equipment he operated hundreds of feet underground. Every day for a week, he reported the machine's defects to his supervisors. An underground miner, Lambert used the machine to drill the holes into which other miners would insert blasting charges. Because there was no proper floor, he had to balance himself precariously upon a series of girders as he operated the drill. And since the International Nickel Company, better known as Inco, operated the mines around the clock, each day two other miners were using the same machine and making the same reports to the foreman. But nothing was going to be done. Time and money spent on maintenance was time and money not spent on production. Nothing ever was done until someone got injured. So Lambert fixed that. "I took a wrench, and I hit my hand as hard as I could. My thumb swelled up, I reported it and I got workers' compensation, and at that point they fixed it."

Working for Inco cost Lambert, who went on to become the Canadian Union of Public Employees health and safety director, part of a finger and some of his hearing and left him with recurring back problems. Inco also turned him into a health and safety activist.

> You are in a completely foreign environment when you go underground. Your sight suffers because you are looking out with a small

29

lamp on your head. You have lost all your peripheral vision. It is impossible to hear underground. No matter where you go there is usually noise all around you. Air escaping from compressor hoses, drills running, huge machines running. You are at a disadvantage right away. The most pressing concerns for most of us were roof falls. We had a number of fatalities during the time that I was there, people working at the face after blasting had gone, as they were working there the roof would cave in from above.

In addition to these problems are the dangers of being run over by a front-end loader, and breathing the diesel fumes that turned the air blue and the oil mist that is now recognized as a cancer-causing agent. In the smelters, workers would be so badly affected by the sulphur in the air that they would be bleeding from the nose.

From 1967 to 1976, 1,670 Canadian miners died from work-related injuries. (This figure is an underestimation of the real effect, since it doesn't include diseases that were not recognized as work-related.) The death rate in mining was ten times higher than in manufacturing. And in the 1970s, as companies like Inco began to invest more money in technology, the injury rate began to soar. Inco had the highest injury rate of any Ontario mining company. The miners knew mechanization did not have to increase injuries, but for that to happen the company had to put safety before productivity. Drills without mufflers were more productive, scooptrams with enclosed cabs to protect the operator and provide a source of clean air were more expensive, and the company had little interest in improving ventilation even as it introduced a fleet of diesel-fuelled equipment to the mines.[1]

As the local chair of the United Steelworkers' Health and Safety Committee, Lambert dealt with an endless series of issues. According to Lambert there was never any progress without a fight. "I remember the battle to get toilets underground—a fairly simple thing—you may not consider it a health and safety issue, but it certainly is when you are expected to squat in a tunnel and crap." He said there was a two-year battle to get Royal Flushes and that victory only came after the miners succeeded in making it a public health—as opposed to an occupational health—issue by raising concerns about the spread of germs to miners' wives.

Stories like these explain why the Canadian health and safety movement first took off in the hard-rock mines of Northern Ontario. From the 1960s onwards the Steelworkers aggressively pursued health and safety issues in these mines, establishing worker-management health and safety committees long before they were required by law. The northern mines were the scenes of illegal strikes, raucous demonstrations, and ongoing conflict. In the end the miners had dug the foundations for a new health and safety system. But the turning point came at Elliot Lake.

A uranium-mining community 140 kilometres west of Sudbury, Elliot Lake boomed in the 1950s when the U.S. military's hunger for uranium led to a rapid expansion of production. However, when the U.S. did not renew its contracts, the town's population dwindled from 25,000 to 6,600. In the 1970s, the nuclear power industry revived the town's economy, bringing thousands of new miners to town.

As is often the case in a one-industry town, neither the miners nor the local business community wanted to hear that it was also home to the most dangerous mines in Canada; but that was Homer Seguin's message. The United Steelworkers' representative in Elliot Lake in the 1970s, Seguin started working for Inco in Sudbury when he was 16 years old. "I operated under the illusion at that time, as many do, that the government would look after me." It was an attitude that he soon lost, but he would encounter it again and again in his work in Northern Ontario. "The people at Elliot Lake went there and they found jobs and had homes, and a lot of people preferred to believe the government and the company, who said there is no problem. When you talked about potential problems that were threatening their lives they wanted to believe it was not killing them."

By the early 1970s many miners began to develop diseases related to the radiation and dust that they were exposed to in the Elliot Lake mines. Said Seguin, "We had people working in their first jobs, and they were becoming silicotic after three years of employment." Governments and employers denied that there was any connection between the diseases and the work in the mines. But under union pressure the Ontario government finally conducted an epidemiology study. This is essentially a body count: a study that looks at the causes of death for a group of workers and then compares them to the general population. The 1975 study results were shocking. According to Seguin, "the epidemiology studies showed that three times as many workers in the uranium mines were getting lung cancer as was expected from the Ontario population." The issue was further inflamed because the study results were not released at Elliot Lake but at an international medical conference in France. "There was unbelievable anger. A lot of people found it hard to believe that the government would first do a study and not tell them about it, then release it in a foreign country—hoping that we would not learn about it back here."

The outraged miners went on the first of many illegal work stoppages. "They put a coffin at the corner of where you turn into the mine. That was the sign that nobody was to work." Seguin said at one point there was a wildcat strike every weekend. Seguin has never accepted that the wildcat strikes were illegal even though they clearly violated the existing labour laws, which prohibited strike action when a contract was in effect. "I am strongly committed to the idea that when things are so bad that you cannot rely on the government and nothing works but the threat of withholding your work you are justified to do it." Ontario New Democratic Party leader Stephen Lewis turned the issue into a *cause célèbre*, visiting Elliot Lake, meeting with the silicotic workers and raising the issue repeatedly in the provincial legislature.

The Ontario government responded by appointing University of Toronto engineering professor James Ham to head up a one-person Royal Commission into the health and safety of Ontario mine workers. The unions pressed home their advantage. Ham described the hearings as a personally radicalizing experience. As he travelled from mining town to mining town diseased workers told him how their jobs had blighted their lives. Activists like Lambert and Seguin recounted their experiences trying to get the mining companies to improve underground health and safety and of their dissatisfaction with government regulation and enforcement. Ham's 1976 report agreed with the unions and the workers; they had been kept in the dark, they had been lied to, and they were dying at excessive rates from a variety of work-related diseases. The minority Conservative government of the day brought in a new health and safety act in 1976 and strengthened it two years later.

Two weeks after the act came into effect, the federal government ruled that it did not apply to the Elliot Lake miners because of a technicality—since uranium was of such importance to national policy, uranium miners were under federal jurisdiction. To add insult to injury, the Atomic Energy Control Board and Labor Canada adopted the previous Ontario mining act regulations. It was not until the government was faced with the threat of strike action in 1994 that AECL agreed to apply the Ontario laws to uranium miners. Two years later the mines closed. The first lung cancer claim for workers' compensation from an Elliot Lake worker was won in 1975. Since then about five hundred more have been accepted as being work-related, and another five hundred have been rejected. Over the years the Steelworkers union forced the government to loosen the criteria for accepting workplace disease claims, although this process was reversed by the Harris government. And while the mines may have closed, the suffering continues. Homer Seguin points to epidemiological studies that make it clear that the rate of mining-related lung cancer among former Elliot Lake workers will continue to rise until the year 2013. "We will be in the mid-2000s before you could eliminate the deaths from lung cancers from Elliot Lake workers."

The American Solution

THE WORKPLACE ACTIVISM THAT led to the adoption of new health and safety laws in Ontario and other provinces was part of a continent-wide movement that linked labour activists and environmentalists and at times pitted workers who were concerned with the nature of their working lives against union leaders who had long been concentrating on simply improving wages and benefits. And just as in Canada, the energy behind that movement was initially generated by miners. In 1969 over 44,000 West Virginia coal miners staged an illegal strike, demanding government compensation for black lung, a fatal disease that struck down coal miners. The miners went on to win a number of important legislative battles, and eventually the rank-and-file health and safety activists took control of the United Mineworkers of America.[2] Following their success, the movement spread to other workplaces and other unions.

This movement was driven in part by the revelations being made by the early environmental movement. When Rachel Carson, in her book *Silent Spring,* revealed the dangers to migratory birds from long-term exposure to low amounts of DDT, workers who made DDT began to ask what was happening to them. Workers were beginning to realize that while they were helping people live better through chemistry, as the advertising slogan of the day put it, the chemicals they were exposed to on the job might have deadly long-term implications.

The health and safety movement in the U.S. was local and community-based, bringing together rank-and-file workers and young professionals and activists who had been radicalized through their opposition to the war in Vietnam. Across the country they formed local Committees on Occupational Safety and Health, or COSHes. According to historian and activist Dan Berman, this new movement began to challenge much of the conventional wisdom that surrounded official occupational health and safety. The health and safety regime that had come into being in the early years of the twentieth century focused on safety issues, held that workers and employers had similar interests when it came to health and safety, and sought to use the workers' compensation system to address the social problems created by workplace accidents. Under this model workers were seen largely as the cause of the problems that arose in the workplace. Programs aimed at reducing injuries often focused on increasing employer control over workers.

The health and safety activists of the 1960s and 1970s turned this way of thinking on its head. Thanks to the work of environmentalists and activist physicians, they recognized that the old system all but ignored occupational disease. People were beginning to realize that cancer, heart disease, and respiratory illnesses may well have their roots in the workplace. Occupational diseases were not a new invention, but in the past employers and governments had been loath to recognize more than a handful of them. The link had to be very clear and apparent, such as the madness that afflicted hatters who inhaled mercury. Workers were slowly becoming aware of the fact that many diseases had a long latency period.

The focus on health issues led workers to realize that employers and employees did not always have convergent interests. Once workers' compensation was introduced, most employers took steps to significantly reduce injury rates, since a lower injury rate for their industry cut a company's compensation bill. Even without this incentive employers would have worked to reduce injuries during the twentieth century, for the simple reason that injuries hurt productivity. Employers and workers may have different motives, but they often both have a keen interest in reducing injuries. This is not the case when it comes to reducing occupational illness. A worker may work productively for years, all the while being exposed to a cancer-causing substance. Often it is only in retirement that the cancer develops. Once they became aware of this, safety activists realized that workers had to become more involved in determining what went on at work and had to know more about the products with which they were working. This critique reflected both the environmental concerns of the day and the growing interest in participatory democracy in Canada and the United States. These concerns would be incorporated to varying degrees in the health and safety laws that were adopted in Canada in the 1970s.

The introduction of medicare in 1968 also led governments to take a greater interest in workplace health and safety. The creation of a universal health care system in Canada significantly increased government health care spending. Much of this money was spent on treating workers who had been injured or made ill on the job. In the mid-1970s federal health minister Marc Lalonde estimated that governments were spending over $750 million treating injured workers. This was a cost the government wanted controlled. Reformed health and safety laws were just another part of the preventive health care measures that Lalonde championed during the 1970s.[3] The first big changes, however, took place in the United States.

PRIOR TO 1970 THERE HAD BEEN little in the way of effective occupational health and safety legislation and enforcement in the United States. It was left to state organizations to regulate workplaces, a task that they often performed in a half-hearted fashion. The 1970 Occupational Safety and Health Act (OSHA) changed that. OSHA was drafted in response to pressure that came from rank-and-file workers who had begun to agitate over a series of local health and safety problems, public interest groups, environmentalists, and unions. It was a part of President Richard Nixon's strategy to win trade union support for his 1972 election campaign—a strategy that was successful, as major union leaders broke with tradition that year and supported the Republicans rather than the Democrats.

The act established a potentially powerful Occupational Safety and Health Administration that had the power to set standards, inspect workplaces and impose penalties on employers who were not complying with the standards. Workers were given the right to participate in inspections, to gain access to information on hazards, and to participate in setting standards. There were also provisions for the criminal prosecution of employers.

Except for a brief burst of activity when Jimmy Carter was president in the late 1970s, OSHA has been a largely moribund agency. It established very few standards, recommended only fifty-seven prosecutions in its first eighteen years, and has never hired anywhere near enough inspectors to make its presence felt in the American workplace. In 1988 OHSA had 2,150 inspectors to cover 5.9 million employers.[4] When Ronald Reagan proclaimed it was once more "Morning in America," he also meant that it was time to pull down the shades on what went on in workplaces. Bill Clinton's New Democrats evinced little interest in reviving OSHA. However, in the 1970s workers in Canada viewed OSHA as a significant accomplishment—they were looking for similar reforms from their own governments.

Bob Sass and the Internal Responsibility System

IN HIS FINAL REPORT HAM RECOMMENDED the creation of what he called an internal responsibility system. He meant that responsibility for health and safety had to be an internal matter for firms. There were too many workplaces, and too many unique circumstances, for government inspectors to use their enforcement powers to create healthy workplaces. However, he also recognized that because management's first priority was production at the lowest cost, it was necessary to give workers a voice in this internal responsibility system. Under the system envisioned by Ham, management would have the responsibility for defining and implementing safety standards, while workers would act as auditors who reported back to management and the government. To improve communications between workers and management, health and safety committees would be created. There was no need to give workers additional power since management and workers had convergent interests when it came to health and safety: "Since both parties desire the good of the individual worker, confrontation can and must be set aside with respect both to accidents and to health-impairing environmental exposures."[5] It is this system, with constant modification, that Canadian workers have been living with for the past twenty-five years.

What was novel about this approach was the degree to which it involved workers in what had up until then been seen as a strictly management matter. Ham that thought this approach was needed to improve efficiency and communications. In devising it, Ham borrowed heavily from the new health and safety laws that had been adopted in Saskatchewan. Those laws were the handiwork of Bob Sass, who had been approaching these issues from a very different perspective.

Bob Sass's father immigrated to New York City from Eastern Europe in 1912 and found work as a window washer. He helped found the Queens and Brooklyn local of the window washers' union, and later went on to be active in the Building Services International Union, now the Service Employees International Union. According to Sass, his father was "very active in the union movement and he was a socialist. So from my early years this was part of my world view."

Sass followed in his father's footsteps, working as a window washer for twelve years. But he also pursued an academic career. After graduating from Hunter College, a part of the City University of New

York, with a degree in English and philosophy, he went to work for the union movement. He started as an organizer for the American Federation of State, County and Municipal Employees (AFSCME) and later became the education and research director for the mammoth Local 91 of the International Ladies Garment Workers Union. Sass also pursued post-graduate studies, getting a degree in industrial relations from Cornell University at Ithaca, New York. This led to his becoming Cornell's director of labour education for central New York State. In 1969, he took a leave of absence to move to Regina to teach labour relations.

Two years later the New Democratic Party won the provincial election and the new labour minister Gordon Snyder, a former railway worker, hired Sass to head the government's mediation and industrial relations branch. In 1973 he was appointed associate deputy minister of labour and given responsibility for reshaping and administering occupational health and safety law in Saskatchewan.

Sass admits that health and safety had never been a major part of his trade union work until that point. During the years that he worked for the AFSCME he had never negotiated a single health and safety clause in any of the union agreements he was involved in negotiating and administering. "At that time," he says, "the thinking in the labour movement was that what we now understand as occupational health and safety, or working conditions—thermal conditions, lighting, noise, dust, chemicals you work with, pace of work—these were considered management prerogatives." In other words, these were not issues over which a union could negotiate. Collective bargaining was restricted to "rates of pay, overtime, holidays, vacation, seniority, bumping rights and so on."

The Canadian labour movement wanted improved health and safety, but the pressure was for stronger regulations and tougher enforcement. Their model was OSHA in the United States. According to Sass, labour wanted "good science [meaning regulations that would set exposure levels at a low enough level that workers would actually be protected], not only that, good science that was enforced. They wanted compliance and they wanted prosecutions used to improve working conditions." Sass was not opposed to labour's position—but his early experiences had convinced him it was not enough. "The policy instruments that labour wanted are totally in the hands of experts." And Sass believed experts were divorced from the sort of knowledge that workers developed about the health and safety hazards of their jobs.

In coming to this conclusion, Sass has been deeply influenced by his efforts to win workers compensation benefits for a Regina worker. George Smith, the president of the Regina Labour Council and a member of the Oil, Chemical and Atomic Workers, approached Sass because he believed that he and five other co-workers at the Saskatchewan Power Corporation were suffering from mercury poisoning as the result of on-the-job exposures. Smith had been hospitalized in 1971 for chronic mercury poisoning and his co-workers were showing symptoms of mercury exposure. However, Smith was denied workers compensation because there was no proof that the poisoning was work related.

Sass told Smith that he did not have any background in the medical and scientific disciplines that shape health and safety. Smith was not to be put off. He had studied mercury poisoning and his own symptoms and was convinced that he was suffering from it. Sass agreed to do what he could. His first problem was finding an expert on heavy metal poisoning who did not work for a major corporation. In the end he was forced to bring in a British physician, Dr. Lesley Euinton, a former British factories medical inspector. Euinton met with the men and then told Sass that he believed that the men not only had suffered mercury poisoning, they were still suffering from mercury poisoning.

> I said to Euinton "How is that possible that you can come up with that determination after George and five others were turned down by a medical review panel unanimously who are considered our occupational health experts?" And then he proceeded to say that, one, there was a problem in terms of their diagnosis. They had low mercury in the urine, which also meant because they were working with it, the body was retaining it. So he went through this series of tests and there was a problem of interpretation—which is

key to all occupational health, it is also subject to interpretation as opposed to science. When he met with them collectively he found out that some of them were experiencing certain symptoms that their individual doctors had never recorded, nor had they said something about, such as impotence. I went through this whole discussion and I was really quite moved. I began to learn a little about how science works in occupational health and safety and how workers experience it.

The learning was not over. Thanks to Sass's pressure, a compensation board medical review panel was convened. Despite Euinton's evidence, the request for compensation was once more denied.

And this of course, you would say was an epistemological crisis for me. Being trained in the social sciences myself, I, too, had a lot of confidence in the scientific discourse. I, too, embraced the notion of empiricism, that you raised a propositional way of knowing and then this propositional thinking is tested by experiment or observation and to the degree that you can reproduce your experiments it would have a high degree of validity.

But he was now confronted with six men whose lives showed him how worker knowledge and experience was ignored by the occupational heath and safety establishment. In this particular case, the Saskatchewan Compensation Board eventually ruled in the workers' favour, but for Sass the role of science and experts was now on the table. "I think as a result of that I put much greater emphasis on the strengthening and deepening of workers' rights in work environment matters."

Another strong advocate of increasing worker rights in the health and safety system was former Saskatchewan Federation of Labour President Bill Gilbey. He was a member of a department of labour study group that helped formulate the Saskatchewan approach to occupational health and safety. And the report that came from that probe on occupational health recommended a joint committee approach to occupational health and safety.

There was also a budgetary rationale for creating a health and safety regime based on worker rights. "We knew we did not have enough technical staff. We were not gong to have enough inspectors, we were not going to have the back-up; whether it was hygiene or occupational physicians and so on." Workers were going to be barefoot technicians. Their knowledge and expertise would be used to police the workplace. In future years this argument could, and did, turn the three rights into a Trojan Horse. Budget cutters would later argue that there was no need for more inspectors or inspections, since the three rights gave workers and their employers the tools they needed to keep workplaces safe.

Sass's legacy was two-fold. First, he centralized all government branches dealing with health and safety into one branch. Mine safety, to give one example, would no longer be the responsibility of Mines and Resources—a department whose priority lay in getting minerals out of the ground, not keeping miners safe.

The second was the creation of the three rights. These are the right to participate, the right to know and the right to refuse. But in Saskatchewan the rights were not introduced as a package. First came the right to participate. The 1972 Saskatchewan Occupational Health and Safety Act mandated the creation of a joint health-and-safety committee for all workplaces with more than ten employees. These committees had no powers and no clear rights. Instead, workers were to bring their problems to the committees, which included an equal number of representatives from management and labour, where they would be discussed.

The second right—the right to refuse work that the worker believes to be dangerous—was introduced in 1973. This was a right that many trade unions, particularly mining unions, had been pressing for. It was meant to bring to an end the situation where a worker who refused to do unsafe work could be disciplined for insubordination. The Saskatchewan government also brought in regulations that provided workers with improved rights to know about the substances with which they were working. Many products that Saskatchewan workers were exposed to were manufactured and packaged outside of the province. For this reason, it was felt that right-to-know legislation would not be effective unless it was nation-wide in scope. As a result, right-to-know legislation did not come into effect in Canada until the late 1980s, in the wake of one of the largest occupational health and safety strikes in the country's history.

The rights were meant as a counterbalance to the deficiencies in the existing health and safety regime. And Sass came to see them as being inter-related. "None could operate without the other." In this vision the right to participate initially included "monitoring, surveillance, inspecting near misses, being able to participate on committees, to come in after work and still be paid, and to have training." The right to refuse work that the worker believed to be dangerous was seen as the equivalent to the right to strike, although this right had to be exercised by workers individually rather than collectively as in a strike. While Sass did not personally accept the argument that workers and employers had identical interests in matters of health and safety, the act he helped develop incorporated this assumption into the committee structure when it did not provide the committees with the power to have their decisions enforced. This has been the case with every jurisdiction that adopted the internal responsibility system. Matters that were not resolved at one meeting were to be referred to the next meeting. If the worker and the management representatives could not come to an agreement, the matter could remain unresolved. But even if the committee did agree on a solution to an issue, management was not required to implement the recommended changes.

These changes did not meet with extensive political opposition in Saskatchewan, something Sass attributes to the fact that there were very few large private-sector employers in the province. The Saskatchewan government had dramatically enlarged the size of the public sector, nationalizing much of the potash mining industry in the province. According to Sass, there were only two private-sector industrial operations with more than five hundred employees. Employers did not fear the early joint health-and-safety committees, although they did have some reservations about the right to refuse, which they felt unions might use to advance collective bargaining as opposed to health and safety issues. At the same time Sass believes the general public did not view these changes as improving the rights of labour as a special interest, but rather as an extension of medicare.

   While the central goal of these reforms was to reduce the severity and frequency of accidents and reduce occupational disease, Sass and others hoped that they would serve to democratize the workplace and to remove health and safety from marketplace regulation. Labour relations is a world of trade-offs in which workers trade time, health, and effort for money. Sass believed that occupational health and safety was different from other labour issues. "It had to be treated differently, as an oasis that would not be governed by management prerogatives whose concern fundamentally was profit." Health and safety was be treated as a good in itself, and the rights attached to it should not be "chopped-up rights to satisfy economic considerations, but should be sort of inalienable rights." Just as it is illegal to sell oneself into slavery in Canada, it should not be possible to sell one's health. It was an admirable goal.

3

THE ETERNAL RESPONSIBILITY SYSTEM

In the 1970s the labour movements all across Canada pushed for the three rights in law. Now twenty-five years later it is time to evaluate what have been the actual effects of these rights. And I would say they are exaggerated when it comes to worker health and safety.

—Bob Sass, September 1998

IN APRIL 1988, BRUCE LIVESEY, a reporter sympathetic to the labour movement, wrote an article for *Business Journal*, a central-Canadian business publication, telling the story of a mass work refusal at one of the country's largest manufacturing plants. At the outset of a nuanced and informative treatment of how over three thousand McDonnell Douglas workers stayed off the job for five weeks to protest unhealthy working conditions, Livesey made an optimistic prediction. He wrote, "the month-long showdown sent a clear message to Canada's corporate community: hazardous working conditions are less likely to be tolerated by employees and will arise on bargaining tables and shop floors."[1] Optimism is the labour reporter's stock-in-trade—no one could cover this world of exploitation, failed strikes and betrayed dreams without a trained eye for the silver-lined cloud over the horizon. As it turned out the McDonnell Douglas work refusal was not the flashpoint for a new round of militancy. In retrospect, it was the high-water mark of the occupational health and safety movement that had its roots in the 1960s.

Through the 1970s and 1980s governments across Canada adopted some version of the legislative model that Bob Sass had been advocating. In some cases, the governments acted out of social democratic principle, in others, such as Ontario, a Conservative minority government was trying to woo the labour vote, and in yet others governments were looking for ways to regulate the workplace without paying for any more inspectors.

Whatever the factors that led to their development, these reforms created tremendous opportunities for Canadian workers, who began to explore their new rights, discover their limitations, and by applying their own ingenuity, use the rights in ways that had not been contemplated by lawmakers. Health and safety conferences became commonplace, and the media regularly reported on occupational health and safety issues. Yet today many observers are in agreement that while the three rights were an improvement over what had existed before, they have failed to bring about the types of changes that many had expected.

A report written by the leading health and safety officials in the Canadian labour movement concluded in 1996 that the system on which they had pinned their hopes was in crisis. The authors of the *New Strategies* report wrote:

> Workers are being forced to become quasi-regulators or peace officers in their own workplaces—without being able to impose a fine or penalty on employers who violate the law and put their health and safety at risk. Through this, their involvement in health and safety committees becomes a constant struggle against co-option by the employer. Employers consistently argue that the "co-operative approach" mandates union health and safety representatives to find ways to achieve compliance from their membership rather than from their employers.[2]

Instead of giving workers more power, it appeared that the system was turning a few workers into representatives of the boss. What had gone wrong?

The Impact of the IRS

It is very difficult to determine if the new laws had any impact on accident rates. Provincial workers' compensation boards are the main source of information on workplace health and safety but they essentially report on compensated injuries and illnesses. As more provinces move to an experience rating system, under which individual firms see their compensation board rates go up with their accident rate, more questions are raised about the reliability of compensation board statistics. It is true that experience rating provides firms with an incentive to reduce accidents. But it also provides them with an even greater incentive to discourage workers from reporting any accidents. This is not idle speculation. A few years ago I was speaking with a labour studies student who working on a project to reduce back injuries at a local warehouse and freighting operation. He had been perplexed to discover that one of this company's American branches had no reported back injuries. Then he discovered that the secret of their success did not lie with superior training or technique: in fact workers were throwing their backs out as frequently as they were at any other plant. But in this case, injured workers were put on light duties rather than workers' compensation. In some cases the duties might not be much more than sitting around the lunchroom playing cards. It was cheaper for the company to keep paying the men than face increased compensation costs. This should not be seen as a humane policy: at some point these workers could become so badly injured that they could not work any more, but they would be unable to point to a history of work-related injuries. And that history is often crucial in establishing a long-term disability claim.

The picture is further muddied by changes in Canada's economic structure. Canada has been losing resource and manufacturing jobs and creating service industry jobs. This shift is likely to lead to a reduction in injuries even if the remaining manufacturing jobs are no safer than they were before. The statistics show that there has been a slight decline in the number of injuries between 1970 and 1996, but injuries may be becoming more severe. In 1970, 38 percent of compensated injuries were ones that were severe enough to require the worker take time off work. In 1996 that figure had risen to 48 percent.[3] Accident rates, in other words, remain high. In 1991 two Winnipeg sociologists surveyed 533 people in Winnipeg about workplace injuries. Fourteen percent of those who had worked the year before reported being injured on the job in the previous year. Fifty-eight percent of those injured missed one or more days of work. It should be noted that less than half of those who were injured filed a claim with the compensation board.[4]

The scene is even more disturbing when one considers the current rates of occupational disease in this country. While workers' compensation board statistics underestimate the number of accidents, they are all but useless when it comes to measuring occupational disease. It is very difficult to prove conclusively that a disease is the result of a workplace exposure or practice. Often a worker may have been exposed to a cancer-causing agent at more than one job or at home as well as at work. In such circumstances the worker may be denied benefits because it cannot be established that the workplace exposure was the dominant cause of the illness. Many workers and their physicians may not even be aware that the worker was at one time exposed to asbestos or cutting fluids or one of the many cancer-causing substances in the workplace. In these situations no claim is even made with the provincial compensation board. Researchers have been able to determine roughly what percentages of various illnesses are likely to be work related. Working from these formulas Dr. Allen Kraut, a physician with the Manitoba Federation of Labour's Occupational Health Centre, calculated that in 1989 between 77,900 and 91,400 Canadian workers developed occupationally related diseases. These could range from dermatitis to cancer. But that wide range should not provide much comfort: Kraut estimated that between 2,052 and 5,130 Canadians died that year as a result of occupational disease. Kraut ended his paper with a cautionary note— because he had not included a number of chronic disorders in his study, it was likely that he actually underestimated the degree of occupational disease in Canadian society.[5]

BEFORE WE TURN TO AN EXAMINATION of the shortcomings of the three Rs, it is extremely important to note that while the rights currently apply to almost all Canadian workers, only about three in ten workers have a realistic opportunity to use those rights. These are the workers who belong to trade unions. It is only in a unionized setting that workers regularly feel comfortable enough to challenge the employer on issues such as health and safety—and to a large degree these are the only workers who are likely to even be aware of their rights. Non-unionized workers are particularly reluctant to make use of the right to refuse unsafe work. One study of the right-to-refuse showed that in the 1980s non-union workers made only 2.9 percent of the refusals, even though they account for 72.2 percent of the workforce.[6]

Ken Bondy, a health and safety activist in Windsor, Ontario, started his working career in a dirty and toxic non-union tool-and-die shop. Shortly after he was hired, an Ontario ministry of labour official came by to inspect the shop. He discovered that, in violation of the law, there was no plant health-and-safety committee. Instead of laying any charges against the company for violating the law that lies at the very heart of the current health and safety regime, the inspector merely ordered that a committee be struck. This may have been a fair exercise of discretion—but it should be noted that no employer has ever been prosecuted or fined for failing to establish a health and safety committee.

And many empoyers simply did not create committees. According to Eric Tucker, a law professor and legal historian specializing in occupational health and safety, in 1984 63 percent of unionized employees were likely to have access to a health and safety committee, while only 32 percent of non-unionized employees had access to a committee in their workplaces.[7] The situation did not improve significantly over time. In Manitoba in 1995 only 29 percent of the firms that were required to have health and safety committees were submitting minutes to the provincial government as required by law. By the end of the century, or twenty-five years after Manitoba's health and safety law had been initially adopted, that figure had risen to 89 percent. During that period no firm had been prosecuted for failure to establish a committee or submit minutes.[8]

Meanwhile, Ken Bondy, working in the non-union tool-and-die shop, had become the new committee's worker co-chair. He soon had an issue that he wanted investigated: the impact that cutting-fluid mists were having on workers. He tried to make the committee system work:

> Over a matter of a couple of days workers began to feel lightheaded. There were workers that began to bleed from the nose when they went home at night. And so in my capacity as the health and safety person I went in and made a complaint to the management and was promptly told to get out of the office and there was nothing wrong and I should not be in there complaining.

On his break he phoned the department of labour. He was told that since he did not a have union representative to handle the case, he should come down to the ministry office and sign a complaint. Bondy said he would be fired if the did that.

> They told me that that could not be the case because it is against the law to fire somebody if they put in a complaint. I said the separation papers are not going to say I was let go because I put a complaint in to the ministry, they will find some other reason. They told me that then there was nothing they could do for me.

Bondy chose to leave the plant shortly afterwards for a job with a unionized company. While many today argue that the three rights are weak rights, it should be remembered for many, if not most Canadian workers, they are really non-rights. Employers can go decades without setting up a health and safety committee, secure in the knowledge that they will not be prosecuted if they are caught. If they have a committee, they know that they can blithely ignore any requirements for submitting minutes. And workers who consider exercising any of their rights, particularly the right to refuse unsafe work, have the threat of the sack hanging over their heads. With no union to back them up financially, it may not be worthwhile to try and get their job back.

BUT HOW DO UNIONIZED WORKERS, the workers who are best able to assert those rights without fear of reprisal, actually experience these reforms? In 1991 a team of academics from McMaster University led by Vivienne Walters conduced a survey of management and union representatives on joint health-and-safety committees. What they discovered was not terribly encouraging to anyone who had hoped that the health and safety committees would lead to a democratization of the Canadian workforce. Worker co-chairs, they reported, often "work closely with management and strongly identify with its concerns about unnecessary [workers' compensation claims]." In at least one instance this extended to even giving workers inaccurate information about their chances of receiving compensation if they were responsible for an accident.[9]

> Workers' representatives were seen as having been co-opted by management, helping to discipline workers. They had become "the policeman," "the bad guy." For their part, the representatives expressed frustration with workers. The links between them were not always strong and supportive.[10]

The committees paid little attention to work organization, while a great deal of effort was focused on worker responsibility. Time was spent stamping out horseplay and ensuring that workers obeyed the rules. While no one wants to see workers put themselves at risk, it appears that many committee members subscribed to the "village-idiot theory" that saw the careless worker as the main problem in the workplace.

While many committee members believed they did a good job in addressing hazards, they were also cautious in how they identified hazards. Safety issues would be given a much higher priority than health threats. Nor were workers pushing the committees. Individually and collectively workers, at the start of what was to turn out to be a calamitous recession, were worried about layoffs, plant closures and being labeled troublemakers. Through experience, worker representatives on the committees had come to know how an inspector would assess an issue. And if they believed an inspector would find a hazard to be acceptable they would not act. Walters' group wrote:

> One top manager said that health and safety had been depoliticized and that management was now "treating every issue as a pure health and safety issue and getting on with it. So we've got the right kind of attitude." He added that once the structure is in place for a

system of internal responsibility, "then you start to deal with the real issues on a straightforward basis, not imaginary issues."[11]

From the employer's perspective—and from government's—these are all signs of maturity and cooperation based on a shared understanding. Health and safety has been tamed and saved from the dangerous adversarial approach that had begun to appear in the 1970s. But in large measure this is because the workers had come to adopt the employer's perspective on what is economically acceptable.

The Westinghouse Story

SO WHAT HAPPENED? AT THE OUTSET, the new laws gave the green light to health and safety activists across the country. Committees were formed, activists were trained, and rights were exercised. There were moments when it appeared the health and safety movement would actually make good on its promise to challenge some of the most fundamental aspects of our economic system. And perhaps one of the best places to go to get a picture of this rank and file rebellion is the huge Westinghouse plant in Canada's industrial heartland, Hamilton.

Over 1,800 people worked at Westinghouse's three Hamilton plants in the early 1980s, making everything from consumer electronics to huge transformers. Among them was Stan Gray, who was to become one of the most celebrated and reviled figures in Canadian occupational safety-and-health history. A former university lecturer from Montreal, Gray moved to Hamilton in the early 1970s in the wake of the crackdown on young radicals following the imposition of the War Measures Act in 1970. While Gray never lost his political perspective, he was re-launched into the world of politics by a crane accident that almost killed a worker. Gray attended a local union meeting, spoke out on what he saw as the company's lack of concern for worker health, and wound up on the health and safety committee. And while he was excited by the new opportunities that the health and safety laws offered, he quickly concluded that there was a huge difference between the law as it existed on paper and the way it was enforced. "The government inspectors were very, very reluctant to enforce their own laws," he said. "Now, the companies perceived that and they did not feel that they had an obligation to change, even where there were legal violations."

Lack of enforcement is a problem that workers have had to grapple with since the first health and safety laws were passed. In the summer of 1908 the *Voice*, a Winnipeg labour paper, ran a headline reading "A Factory Act Which is Good to Read, but Otherwise Good for Nothing." The outrage was sparked by the death of Percy Santler, the secretary of the Elmwood branch of the Amalgamated Carpenters and Joiners Union. He died when a large piece of timber became stuck in a circular saw he was working at the Brown and Rutherford plant in Winnipeg and was hurled against his chest. He was the second man to die of such an injury in two years in that factory. "The Manitoba Factory Act stipulates that all machinery shall be guarded, but this provision has not been interpreted to require the guarding of these circular saws."[12] A year later the Labour Council still was reporting that "the inspector has not devoted his whole time to the work."[13] There was more to this than laziness. W.G. Carson, in a history of factory inspection, shows that almost from the outset inspectors were supposed to persuade rather than prosecute. In 1849 British factory inspectors were instructed to:

> Show, by close examination, that obedience to the Act and compliance with the regulations of the Inspectors will be required; but endeavour, as much as possible, to effect this by explanation, respectful admonition, and warning: make it evident that when you find things wrong, you do so with regret…"[14]

The inspector's role in Victorian England was to approach the employer respectfully, cap in hand, and ever so politely ask if they could have a bit more compliance with the law. One did not prosecute gentlemen.

These sentiments could still be found in the annual reports of the Manitoba Department of Labour in the 1950s. Indeed the reformers of the 1960s had wanted tougher laws and stricter prosecution along with enhanced worker rights. What they got was a system in which the enhanced rights were too often used as an excuse to cut back on enforcement. Under the IRS philosophy, workers and employers have supposedly been given the tools that they need to address workplace health and safety issues. In the joint committees an equal number of worker and employer representatives meet, often on a monthly basis, to discuss workplace concerns. They are the ones who know the workplace and what needs to be done. Better they work out solutions cooperatively than have outside inspectors enforce inappropriate rules on both workers and employers. The inspector is meant to take on the role of facilitator who will, according to the Ontario ministry of labour's manual for health and safety inspectors, "identify, evaluate and review the actions of labour and management on a regular basis."[15]

There is a lot to be said for this approach. Workers and employers do have the clearest idea of what is going on in the plant, although they may not fully understand the health implications of certain substances and work practices. But to go back to Bob Sass's pertinent comment: power is power. And joint health-and-safety committees in Canada are purely advisory; they have no power. Furthermore, because they are joint committees, half of the members being from the workforce, half from management, it is very difficult to imagine a situation where a committee might come up with a recommendation that would require management to spend a considerable amount of money on health and safety against its will.

The inspector's role is to act as a facilitator, bringing the members of the health and safety committee together to develop common solutions to their problems. An inspector who starts hauling one of the parties into court on a regular basis is soon going to lose his or her ability to act as a facilitator.

Gray and his co-workers soon ran up against these limitations. And they began to find ways to work around them. One of the first tests for the new system was a band saw whose blades kept breaking. The union raised the matter with the company and the inspector, but in each case were told there was nothing wrong with the saw. Nor could they get any support from an inspector.

They turned to guerrilla warfare, making creative use of a provision in the health and safety act requiring workers to inform their employer of any workplace hazards. As soon as the morning shift came on duty, one worker went to see his supervisor to alert him to the existence of an unsafe band saw. The supervisor told him the saw had been checked out and was fine. The worker went back to work. But fifteen minutes later, twenty-five workers were outside the supervisor's door, each of them prepared to report the unsafe saw. Fifteen minutes after the supervisor got them all back to work, the entire department walked off the job. Gray spoke on their behalf.

> I say, "listen we just want to make sure you are aware and report you an unsafe band saw." He says, "I already told you that band saw is safe—go back to work." We say, "fine, we just want to make sure you are aware, we have an obligation under the law to report an unsafe hazard."

> The manager at one point perceived that he is losing a fortune in production time. That what we were doing was perfectly legal. Before lunch at twelve o'clock, he had that band saw removed from the plant, and ordered a new one. He ordered the maintenance department, to cut the bolts on the saw. It had become a red flag to people. He could not get any production out of that department as long as that band saw was there. Even though the inspector had said it was OK, even though management had refused to fix it, he had to remove that saw within hours in order to get production out of that plant.

It was a victory for direct action. But Gray was soon to discover that it was going to be very difficult to make the new legislation live up to its billing. In late November 1979 a 45-gallon drum exploded at the Westinghouse Beach Road plant. Terry Ryan, a 22-year-old worker, was robbed of his sight, his senses of smell and taste, and left with a variety of health problems. An investigation indicated that the drum contained toluol, a highly volatile solvent. The drum, which was supposed to contain products used to clean transformers, should not have had any toluol in it.

In less than a month the Ontario government inspectors concluded that while it was not possible to discover what caused the explosion, no laws had been violated. Gray found this conclusion hard to accept. And making use of new provisions in the Ontario

Health and Safety Act, he launched his own inquiry. By July of the following year he had produced a forty-page report demonstrating that toluol had been used in an unauthorized and illegal fashion throughout the plant. There had been little training about the product, nor were workers provided with the appropriate safety equipment. In particular, he said that the product's improper use was well known by company management. He argued that the company had violated several of the act's provisions. It was at this point, nearly nine months after the accident, that the government laid charges against Westinghouse. There were a number of errors in the charge, which could have led to the case being thrown out of court. However, Gray caught the errors and the charges were laid for a second time.

Even still, the workers never got their day in court. Just before they were set to testify about the working conditions at Westinghouse, the Crown announced that it had reached an agreement with Westinghouse. Six charges were going to be dropped, while the company would plead guilty to a seventh, minor, charge and pay a $5,000 fine.

It was the first shot in what was to be a running battle that had Gray and his fellow workers on one side and Westinghouse and the Ontario government on the other. The conflict would culminate in a hearing before the labour board in which Gray accused the Ontario government inspector of intimidating him and attempting to deny him his rights under the health and safety act. The labour board, in a judgement that symbolized many of the problems with the new health and safety regime, substantiated all of Grays' charges. It also rejected the inspector's explanations for his actions. Despite this, the board ruled in the inspector's behalf. And therein hangs a tale.

TODAY GRAY RUNS A SMALL advocacy business out of a high-rise office building in downtown Hamilton. Much of his work is representing people with workers' compensation claims. The walls of the office feature a number of framed full-page newspaper articles on Gray. Reading them as I waited for our interview, it was apparent that here was a man who relished a fight. Since his years with Westinghouse he's been involved in dozens of workplace health and safety battles.

Throughout his career he's mastered arcane sets of rules and disciplines, and used them to great effect in battles with the establishment.

Gray, who is over six feet tall and spreading, dominates his tiny office. He had dozens of documents for me: articles and letters to the editor he has written; articles about him and his struggles; and more general background. And while some of these battles are more than twenty years old, he had little trouble summoning the details of those events or the passions that accompanied them. He closed his eyes, leaned back his head and brought back to life his long-running conflict with Ontario workplace inspector Lawrence Bergie.

In 1981, in response to worker complaints about air quality in the welding shop, government inspectors performed a number of tests and gave the shop a clean bill of health. The workers continued to complain and stage work refusals, while Gray arranged to have outside experts conduct tests for the union. The consultants concluded that there were unhealthy levels of oxides of nitrogen in the air. Furthermore they said the government officials had been performing inappropriate tests. After a year of conflict, during which Bergie scolded Gray for making use of outsiders, the company agreed to install a new ventilation system in the welding shop.

At the same time, the committee was raising concerns over fumes to which workers were exposed when they worked inside large tanks. Unable to get information from the company through the health and safety committee, Gray put pressure on the ministry for tests. After six months of Gray's agitating, the government tested a cold tank from the outside, even though Gray had been asking for a test on a hot tank from inside. Meanwhile Gray kept raising the issue at health and safety committee meetings. It was not until September 1982, two-and-a-half years after Gray first raised the issue, that the government issued an order that required that the tanks be tested before workers entered them.

One of the key weapons the workers made use of in these skirmishes was the right to refuse unsafe work. Even when the government regulators said the process was safe, the employer was prepared to improve working conditions when faced with the loss of production that a work refusal created. According to Gray, this was a very exciting and dynamic time at Westinghouse. Even if the government was not prepared to enforce the act, the workers had embraced some of its elements, using them to win improvements. But this forward motion was halted by the recession of the early 1980s.

> When you have a recession your shop floor power goes right down because people don't have the instruments to force the companies to change. They don't need your work any more. Instead of people refusing to work, they are fighting to get those jobs because a quarter of the plant is going out the door.

As workers were less willing to take on-the-job action over health issues, Gray and the health and safety committee began to make greater use of the media and opposition political parties. In the early 1980s New Democratic Party labour critic Elie Martel was more than happy to raise health and safety issues up in the legislature. While Martel won the Westinghouse workers considerable publicity, this did not endear them to their employer or the government.

The final collision came when the union began pushing the company over the dangers of lead-based paints. Airborne lead poisoning can cause fatigue, insomnia, headaches, and high blood pressure. Long-term exposures, even at low levels, can be quite dangerous. The Ontario government had issued new exposure limits for lead in the air in the summer of 1981. Industry was supposed to meet these levels by November of that year. November came and went without Westinghouse having introduced a lead-control program that met the new standards. In the spring of 1982—the same time that Gray and company were pressing the company on ventilation in the welding shop and fumes in the tanks—Gray raised the lead issue with the Ontario government. The government ordered the company to carry out tests. When the results of these tests were released it was shown that the lead levels were six times the limit.

Gray was also making sure that the NDP raised the issue in the provincial legislature. Bergie then warned Gray "there'll be trouble" if he gave any more information to the NDP. If that was too cryptic, he also threatened to disband the Westinghouse health and safety committee unless Gray and the other union members abandoned their confrontational approach. During this period the company—in violation of the law—put together a lead-assessment program without union input. For trying to get information on the paints in the company storerooms Gray was given a one-day suspension. While Gray was on the side of the angels, one suspects that he did not take a please-and-thank-you approach to management in these situations.

When the company tests showed that the lead levels were too high, the government conducted its own tests, a move that further angered the workers. As Gray pointed out, the government had never questioned Westinghouse test results that showed the company was in compliance with existing standards. For its part, the company took the position that the tests were being done when the wrong paint was being used. Hydro green was the most commonly used paint and the company was sure that when it was used it would be clear that the levels were safe. As Gray tells it,

> They did a hydro green test. It was twenty times the legal stand-
> ard—twenty times. According to tests done both by the company
> and the government. And still we had no lead-control program.
> And still they refused to order the company to reduce the levels.

Indeed the labour department said the company had "gone beyond the requirement of consultation with the committee to try to reach agreement on the provision of the control programme." The Ontario government's director of health and safety was dispatched to Hamilton. He urged Gray and the other committee members to learn to cooperate and communicate. Gray recalls his attitude then with bemusement:

> Well, I told them, "We would not have called you in if we could
> have had a cooperative solution here. The paint is unsafe, they refuse
> to fix it, so don't tell us to cooperate with the guys who are threat-
> ening our health and safety. You enforce your own law." Well the
> government comes out with their IRS rhetoric, which says, "No,
> no, no, no. Our role is not to enforce anything, our role is just to
> make you guys cooperate." No matter how much you cooperated

with management it would not get the lead out of the paint, it wouldn't get anything fixed.

For this reason, and despite Bergie's warnings, Gray kept up his public campaign. In January 1984 the company announced it would no longer be using lead-based paints. But the story was not over. While Gray believed that Bergie was simply following government policy, a technicality required that Gray file any complaints with the labour board against an individual, as opposed to the department of labour. And so Gray lodged a complaint against Bergie. During the hearings he was able to once more give a public accounting of his efforts to have the Ontario government enforce its health and safety laws.

The labour board accepted Gray's evidence and acknowledged that Bergie had acted improperly when he threatened Gray and the committee. However, it did not rule in Gray's favour. Instead it concluded that it would rule for Bergie because he was attempting to have the committee implement the act's policies. The ruling read in part:

> The hope was, and continues to be, that on matters of health and safety the parties in a unionized institution might be able to divorce themselves from the adversarial approach characteristic of collective bargaining in this jurisdiction.[16]

Under the Internal Responsibility System the role of the inspector was to identify and respond to breakdowns in the system. He should only enforce the law when the internal responsibility system's limits had been reached. And there were no clear guidelines as to what those limits were. For this reason many workers have come to term it the Eternal Responsibility System: issues could remain unresolved for all of eternity. The labour board agreed that Gray knew what he was talking about, that the health hazards were real, but accused him of carrying out his work on the committee with an "uncompromising cynicism" and "an abundant willingness to politic and 'media-tize' his concerns."[17] Gray had gone to the media because the government had not enforced its own laws—something that might well engender no small amount of cynicism on his part.

But his major failing in the labour board's eyes was engaging in behaviour that led to a decrease in cooperation on the joint health-and-safety committee.

Gray had won a moral victory, but his days at Westinghouse were numbered. Along with his ongoing battles with management and government, he was also in conflict with the leadership of his union, the United Electrical Workers. While the UE was known for its left-wing views on a variety of political issues, Gray believed it was not supporting shop floor activists when it came to health and safety. Then the union and the company agreed to a contract provision that limited the length of time a worker could hold a position on the joint health-and-safety committee, effectively removing Gray from the committee. Gray and other workers felt that the company and the union were collaborating to try to stifle the conflict that Gray was generating.

In 1984 the United Steelworkers, following on the lead of the Manitoba Federation of Labour, decided to open up its own occupational health clinic. The impetus for these clinics came from the long and unhappy relationship between workers and company doctors. These doctors often were more concerned with screening out unhealthy job applicants, reducing absenteeism, and fighting workers' compensation claims than with addressing occupational health issues. Indeed, very few Canadian doctors had any training in occupational health prior to the 1980s. In her study of Canadian company doctors in the early 1980s, Vivienne Walters concluded that "most doctors defined their responsibility as one of informing or convincing workers of the 'reasonable' risks to which they are exposed." One physician told her, "We've got to help the operating manager make reasonable decisions about the hazard potential and, having said that on management's side, we've got to fulfill our obligation to the employees and their union—to point out to them that it is indeed a reasonable hazard for them to be exposed to."[18]

The Hamilton Steelworkers offered Stan Gray the job of executive director of the Ontario Workers Health Centre. It was an opportune moment. All across Canada workers were seizing the opportunities that had been created by the new health and safety laws. In coming years, it would appear as if management's worst fears were going to be realized: workers would use health and safety as an issue through which to challenge management's right to manage. The fundamental questions about what was done in the workplace and who did it would end up on the bargaining table.

The Hamilton Clinic was at the centre of many of these controversies, providing workers with access to outside medical opinions and research. Since these researchers had no commitment to "helping the operating manager" keep production up, they often took a less charitable view of the risks workers were being asked to assume. The clinic diagnosed diseases in Burlington chemical workers, asbestos exposure among Hamilton school board workers, and hearing loss problems in a variety of industries. In most cases, both company doctors and the government had ignored these problems. The fact that workers had been kept in the dark created a political problem for the provincial government and employers. This problem became worse as the Ontario economy bounced back from the recession of the early 1980s. As employment increased workers once more began to flex their muscles and exercise the right to refuse unsafe work. In 1986 and 1987 these issues exploded into the two largest work refusals in Canadian history as workers at two of the country's largest aircraft manufacturers walked off the job to protest health hazards.

The Aircraft Work Refusals

THE FIRST EXPLOSION CAME at the de Havilland plant in Downsview, near Toronto. In 1986 the de Havilland local of the Canadian Auto Workers, which also represents workers in the aerospace industry, asked Gray to conduct a survey of health hazards in the de Havilland plant. The workers had been complaining of rashes and burning eyes, and were not satisfied with the answers they were getting from company doctors. The company would not allow Gray to set up a clinic in the factory, so he operated out of the union hall. "We found hundreds of workers exposed to unsafe chemicals," Gray recalls.

People whose lungs were permanently damaged, people who had permanent eye damage, people whose eyes were puffy all day, people who were dizzy from the narcotic properties of those chemicals. People who had extensive skin damage, all from the plastics and paint and chemicals they worked with. The company knew that, the company had documented it, and the company had never told those workers.

One of the major hazards facing the de Havilland workers came from isocyanates, a product that is used in a variety of solvents. It was known to be dangerous—in fact the Ontario government required that companies that use isocyanates have a specific control program for the product. The company had gone years without such a program, despite being told time and again that it had to put one in place. According to Gray, "The company took a signal from that, that the law is just a piece of paper and they continued to violate it with impunity."

When Gray's report was released, it was if a match had been thrown into a field of dry grass. Over six hundred workers refused to work. The ministry of labour sent in inspectors and discovered that de Havilland was not in compliance with the health and safety act. Once more orders were written up, but the company was allowed to set its own timeline for implementation. The workers were outraged. This time there were so many work refusals the plant was shut down for a week. Gray remembers,

> In one week they got an agreement from the company to get rid of some of those chemicals, to put controls on others, to give proper instruction, proper protective equipment. They ended up spending millions of dollars refurbishing that plant. They got more in one week of action than they got in years of begging and pleading.

While Gray's clinic was excluded from the initial agreement that was worked out by the national office of the CAW and de Havilland, the workers eventually insisted that the Ontario Workers Health Centre replace the company physicians. The conflicts that were arising between Gray and the national office of the CAW were reminiscent of his battles with his old union, the UE. To some degree they may have arisen from the way Gray became front and centre in these conflicts—he had a very good working relationship with *Toronto Star* labour reporter John Deverell—but they also reflect the way that health and safety issues can create problems for union leaders.

It turned out that the de Havilland strike was simply the prelude to what was going to happen at McDonnell Douglas. Over 3,400 CAW members worked at the Malton, Ontario McDonnell Douglas plant, turning out wings and tail sections for jet planes. In May of 1987 they elected Nick DeCarlo as president of their union local. Shortly before his election, DeCarlo had been fired by the company, which claimed it had let him go because he had provided false information on his 1979 job application. DeCarlo believes the company was scared of what might happen if he became president. The only thing wrong with his job application was that he had hidden the fact that he had degree in civil engineering and a trade union background.

Interviewing Nick DeCarlo in his modest brick home in downtown Toronto, it is hard to imagine him as a dangerous firebrand who shut down an industry. He is soft-spoken and chooses his words carefully. Where Gray gets swept up in the dramatic events he is recounting, DeCarlo is so matter of fact one almost forgets that he is talking about the largest health and safety strike in Canadian history. One can also miss the inner toughness and determination that has served him so well in a career that has seen him become a CAW environment officer.

His calm demeanour must have served him well fifteen years ago. The de Havilland local of the CAW was, after a long period of quiescence, starting to show signs of life. In the early 1970s the company had fired the union leadership, while the union's then-U.S. based leadership had undercut the workers during a bitter strike. According to DeCarlo the company placed the workers under very tight supervision during this period. "Most people who attempted to buck the system or take on the company were fired or disciplined or moved or transferred. There were all kinds of ways of preventing people from organizing." By the mid-1980s workers were feeling more secure in their jobs and came very close to voting down a contract that had been approved by the union's national office. DeCarlo's candidacy captured the support of those younger workers who were restive with all aspects of McDonnell Douglas management.

Health problems began to come to the fore. "Over time there were things that you would notice. People got sick or would develop cancer or you would notice that a lot of people lost their sense of smell. And you would start to wonder what is it that we are working with that would cause that kind of thing," DeCarlo explained. The fact the ministry of labour had not conducted a thorough plant inspection in over eight years also grated. Needless to say, without inspection there was no enforcement. CAW activists on the health and safety committee were starved for information and unable to get action out of either the government or the employer.

Drawing on the de Havilland experience, one of DeCarlo's first actions was to invite in the Ontario Workers Health Centre. The physicians diagnosed fibrosis (a scarring of the lungs), high level of aluminum in workers' blood, and discovered that the workers, and possibly even their supervisors, did not know about the risks of many of the products they were using. For example, while workers were given data sheets on some products, many of these sheets failed to mention that that the product had been linked to the development of cancer. It was de Havilland all over again. According to DeCarlo, "It went from being an abstract concept, of maybe there is a problem or your health could eventually be affected, to a very real recognition that at that moment people were indeed sick often due to the exposures in the workplace." Workers were particularly disturbed to discover that there was a high percentage of people with memory problems in the plant, since Alzheimer's disease is associated with exposure to aluminum.

The union held regular membership meetings and published a series of leaflets outlining what was being discovered by Gray and the clinic physicians. Still smarting from its public embarrassment at de Havilland, the ministry of labour sent in inspectors in the fall of 1987. After a thirty-seven-day inspection they found over two hundred violations of the health and safety act. McDonnell Douglas was violating regulations in its use of lead, asbestos, mercury, silica and isocyanates. Only a fraction of the workers exposed to these products had received the proper training, while the company had not been keeping individual exposure records or reporting employee illness to the health and safety committee. Finally, they concluded that the plant's ventilation system was "a mess" that often cycled toxins back into the plant.

Again there were no firm deadlines on having these problems addressed. When DeCarlo complained to government officials about the slow pace he was told, "if it is such a problem why aren't you refusing to work." If they were trying to call his bluff, it was a mistake.

On November 18, six hundred McDonnell Douglas workers took the government's advice and refused to work. When union officials arrived at the plant to talk to the workers, who were occupying the lunchroom, management called the police to keep them out. Soon the company, in contravention of the health and safety law, was threatening not to pay those workers who were refusing to work. In short order over three thousand people were refusing to work. DeCarlo says he was stunned by the response. "We no idea it would be as massive as it was." The plant was to shut down for five weeks and McDonnell Douglas was losing $300,000 a day, more than double the entire amount the Ontario government had levied in fines against all employers in the previous year for violating workplace health and safety laws.

The company and the union were in negotiations throughout this period. The company agreed to pay those workers who were refusing to work and made concessions on a variety of health and safety issues. The workers gained a new ventilation system, better control over toxic substances, and improved training. But on New Year's Day the company announced it was going to have to lay off 238 workers for economic reasons. This marked a turning point in the protest. The fear of job loss took the wind out of the protestors' sails. The work refusal came to an end. By the spring of 1988 the company had rectified all but a handful of its two hundred-odd health and safety violations. One of the direct results of the strike was the final adoption of national product safety system know as the Workplace Hazardous Materials Information System, or WHMIS. Government had to give in to the workers' right to know about what they were working with. After years of intergovernmental foot-dragging a national information system was finally brought into effect. This system remains one of the foundations of any meaningful right to know. The de Havilland strike marked a turning point in the history of the occupational health and safety movement.[19] Just not in the direction that labour had expected.

Powerlessness and Bipartism

THE ASPECT OF THE INTERNAL Responsibility System that health and safety activists found most frustrating was the fact that the joint committees were only advisory and yet were made up of an equal number of labour and business representatives. As Cathy Walker, the health and safety director of the Canadian Autoworkers said, "It is ironic that management does not have to act on a recommendation made by a committee to which it appoints half of the members." Len Wheeler, who acted on Bill Quinn's behalf before the Workers' Compensation Board of Manitoba, had been a rail worker when the federal government first adopted the IRS. "I was quite excited about it," Quinn said.

> On paper it looked very, very promising for workers. Finally you were going to be given some protection to say, "No, I don't want to do that, it is dangerous." And you did not have to worry about sanctions. I quickly lost my excitement about it because when you went into the committees and you dealt with management and it was all said and done and came back out on the floor they were the ones with the ultimate decision as to whether what you had just recommended was going to be implemented. You could not force them to implement.

While many workers simply became disillusioned with the process or simply used it to have minor safety issues addressed, the aircraft plant strikes made it clear that there was another response to this powerlessness. As Stan Gray notes, the strikes inspired and educated workers at countless other plants.

> That was an incredible lesson to workers all over the place. It had a dynamic impact, because in every plant in Ontario workers read

all about it, it was on TV all the time, it was in the press, it told them, you don't to have to put up with this crap. There are laws that say you should not have to lose your health at work, you should not have to lose your leg, or your lung, or your liver or your kidney or your brains, or your nose or whatever. That is not part of what going to work means, there are laws that stop that. And if the authorities won't enforce it you can shut the plant down, you have the legal right to refuse. Those workers got paid all the time they were refusing work. You can shut it down, get paid while it is happening, and you have a cleaner plant and a better life as a result.

Workers had taken the tools provided by the internal responsibility system and refashioned them. And in doing so they made it clear just how politically charged workplace health and safety could be. Governments and employers and, in the opinion of some, senior labour leaders, decided to defuse the problem by making even greater use of the joint labour-management approach to health and safety that the joint committees represented. This approach came to be known as bipartism, and in the minds of some health and safety activists, it undermined the health and safety movement.

In Ontario bipartism was enshrined in 1990 in Bill 208. It established a new Workplace Health and Safety Agency complete with a joint worker-manager board of directors. The centre was meant to take the leading role in training workers and managers in health and safety issues. It was through this agency that at least one worker and one employer member of each committee was expected to be trained and certified. A joint committee structure was also put into place to develop exposure standards for many workplace toxins. For many unionists it was an attractive proposition, and with a few exceptions the labour movement embraced the process. One union that did not do so was the Ontario Public Service Employees Union. Its leaders recognized that this approach could in the long run undermine the role that government inspectors—who were OPSEU members—were supposed to play in enforcing health and safety standards. Secondly, OPSEU leaders opposed what they saw as the depoliticizing of the issue. Bob DeMatteo, the union's health and safety director, says that the labour movement was sidetracked by bipartism.

> It became used by the other side, by governments intent on deregulating, for example, and the business communities. When we set up the workplace health and safety agency in the province and said we were going to train our members to do their job out there as certified members, with very little power, I think we set ourselves up for a very bad situation.

Nick DeCarlo was another critic of this approach. He pointed out that by participating in the committees and committing themselves to a process of joint decision making, unions found it very difficult to take issues to the public. "The problem is you have bought into it so you can't really oppose it. If you are outside the process—in a union but you disagree with it—you can criticize but you are working against pretty massive odds." One of the people who was marginalized by these developments was Stan Gray. Under the new bipartite approach a new network of occupational health centres was established. But there was no room for Gray's muckraking approach.

These criticisms are not undisputed. For many years Cathy Walker was the health and safety officer for the Canadian Association of Industrial, Mechanical and Allied Workers (CAIMAW), a feisty union that made it a point of principle not to participate in bipartite arrangements. This principle allowed the union considerable independence of action and speech. Following CAIMAW's merger with the CAW in the 1990s Walker went on to become the CAW's health and safety director. In that position she has won the respect of many health and safety activists in Ontario; as one of them told me, "Cathy Walker walks on water." But she is not apologetic for the union's participation in joint management-labour agencies:

> It did give labour far more opportunity to ensure that workers on health and safety committees had far more health and safety training than they had before. Was it somewhat politically tainted? Was it more conservative than if labour had been putting forward our kind of training in our own forums? Possibly. On the other hand it did give all sorts of people in all sorts of circumstances far more

health and safety knowledge than they had ever had before. I think it was very much a two-edged sword.

One thing you should not forget about in Bill 208, the health and safety act changes in Ontario, it also provided for a one-hour caucus time for the union or worker members on the joint committee to organize their thoughts and their agenda before the joint meeting with management. That is the only jurisdiction in the country that I am aware of that affords that opportunity. It really shows quite graphically, the fact that workers do have a different agenda from management and do need an opportunity to organize their agenda.

Bill 208 also required joint committees in more kinds of workplaces and created a mechanism by which work could be stopped if the certified worker and employer representatives on the committee agreed that it was necessary to do so.

Finally, Walker notes, bipartism, in the form of the joint health-and-safety committee, was built into the current system from the outset. Whether dealing with the plant committee or a province-wide training committee, she feels that labour representatives have to remember there is no difference between sitting down at the bargaining table and sitting down at a health and safety committee table. "And you should conduct yourself in exactly the same way. You should sit down with your group, the labour movement, the workers, and figure out what your agenda is, and go there and try and bargain with management your agenda. And unfortunately often times in these bipartite organizations people forget that there is a worker agenda, there is a union agenda, and that is what they should be pursuing, and not some amorphous joint responsibility."

To some Bill 208 constituted a fatal wrong turn on labour's part. Others believe that union leaders wanted the health and safety movement deactivated simply because wildcat strikes like the ones at de Havilland and McDonnell Douglas were uncontrollable. Others are more likely to blame the recessions of the 1980s and 1990s. But as the following story from Manitoba's meatpacking industry suggests, by the 1990s real change was no longer on the table.

The Killing Floor and the Level Playing Field

FEW WORDS HAVE BEEN more common in business writing over the past two decades than restructuring. We regularly hear that firms, industries, and entire economic sectors are being restructured. Along with downsizing it has been one of the most ubiquitous euphemisms of our time. The "re-" words—renovate, renew, rejuvenate—all carry positive connotations. Who could be opposed to old smokestack industries restructuring themselves, particularly if they take the opportunity to invest in high tech gizmos designed to make work easier and the company more profitable?

One has only to look at the meat packing industry to catch a glimpse of some of the unpleasantness that lurks behind the benign concept of restructuring. Over the last two decades the packing industry has restructured itself with a vengeance. For years three large companies, Canada Packers, Swift's, and Burns dominated the Canadian market, with the smaller J.M. Schneider's running fourth place. By the 1950s these companies had built huge plants in most major Canadian cities. From these two dozen or so plants they supplied the Canadian meat-buying market. And that was a pretty predictable and growing market. Eating red meat was a status symbol, and the more of it you could barbecue in the back yard, the higher your status.

But by the 1980s red meat was under attack. People were switching to chicken and, of all things, to beans and legumes. Mass markets were giving way to niche markets. At the same time Canadian packers found themselves under growing threat from foreign competition. There was nothing to do but restructure. Which meant reducing wages, reducing the size of the workforce, and increasing production. The old plants would be closed and new plants would make use of the latest in high-tech butchering tools. The recession of the early 1980s with its high rates of unemployment gave companies the strength they needed to take on the unions, although they did not give in without a fight.

The modern meat packing industry was created in the closing years of the nineteenth century. In many ways it was the precursor of the assembly line industry that Henry Ford is credited with creating in Detroit. Meatpacking has a disassembly line, rather than an assembly line, but from the outset it had a standard product that was sold to a mass market, a semi-skilled workforce that was divided up into a number of specific jobs, and made use of specialized tools. The old plants, which still stand vacant on the edges of many cities, were multi-storied affairs with the killing floor on the top level. After the animal was killed, its carcass would be gradually disassembled and processed as it was fed by gravity from one floor to the other. The work, as anyone who had read Upton Sinclair's muckraking classic *The Jungle* knows, was always dangerous. Blood and animal fat could leave the floor a slippery mess, the animals presented a variety of dangers (including infection), and if a worker was not wielding a sharp knife in close quarters, he or she was likely to be wrestling a hefty side of beef.

For all its dangers meatpacking was well-paid work. At the end of the Second World War the packinghouse unions had staged a nationwide strike that won them the right to negotiate national contracts. As a result, employers could not try to drive down wages by pitting the workers in one plant against the workers in another. By the 1980s the companies had concluded that the system of nationwide bargaining had to go. In 1984 Burns faced its workers in a lengthy strike and ended the negotiating of national contracts. At the same time Canada Packers, after a shorter strike, won the right to institute a different wage system in each of its plants.

The companies were now paying less for their labour. And they began to upgrade their facilities. Most of the old multi-story plants were closed, with a loss of well over five thousand jobs. Instead, the companies began to focus on single-story plants that operated with a single purpose. In the past plants had often processed beef and pork under one roof. Now it was more likely that a plant would be dedicated to a single animal and a few products. In these plants management could extend its control and reduce worker autonomy. Wherever possible the work would be driven by machines. This has not been as easy in the packing industry as in other sectors. No two animals are exactly the same, therefore much of the work still has to be performed by hand—or more accurately by hand-held knives and power tools. Wherever possible the packers have introduced more disassembly lines, reduced the number of jobs that an individual worker does from start to finish, and cranked up the line speed. Where once ham-boners stood at a stationary tabled and individually dressed a ham every four minutes, there is now a conveyor belt. Workers on either side of the belt perform only a few specific cuts on a ham before it moved on.

From 1984-87 the Burns plant in Winnipeg doubled its hog kill. At the new rate of 440 hogs an hour, workers had eight seconds to make their cut and get on to the next one. This rate increase was implemented with no increase in the number of people working on the line.

By cutting the wage rates the company also increased the staff turnover. The result was that there were more untrained people working in the plants, and fewer experienced workers to show them the ropes. Joel Novek, a University of Winnipeg sociologist, studied the health and safety implications of these changes and concluded that:

> Mechanization has done little to reduce the risks associated with meat packing. In fact, by enabling packers to step up the pace at which animals are killed and processed, it has made things worse. Packers have responded to the challenge of labour intensity by attempting to step up output to the highest possible level. This means that workers must work faster performing tasks which are increasingly machine paced, repetitive, and technically controlled.[20]

At the Burns Winnipeg plant the accident rate rose from 25.8 lost time accidents per hundred workers in 1983 to 39.4 per hundred in 1986. The Burns workers had seen the future and it hurt. A five-minute drive away was one of the last of the old multistory plants. Run by Canada Packers, this plant had a much lower accident rate (18.1 lost-time accidents in 1986 compared to 39.4 at Burns), fewer grievances, and less turnover. Novek wrote:

> While many factors must be considered when comparing and analysing workplace injury rates, the contrasts in claims between one plant undergoing intensified production in an atmosphere of la-

bour-management discord and a second plant subject to a less intense labour process, deserves to be taken seriously.[21]

But while the Canada Packers plant may have been safer, it was not competitive. Workers were forced to make a choice between their jobs and their health. Canada Packers had not intensified the labour process at its Winnipeg plant because it was planning to close it down. It made the announcement in December of 1986, and by October of 1988 the plant was an empty shell and a thousand people had lost their jobs.

The story of the "successful" restructuring of the Canadian meat packing industry, where wages were pushed down while injury rates and profits rose underscores Canadian poet Tom Wayman's views on productivity. In his poem "Defective Parts of Speech: Official Errata," Wayman proposes that the word "suffering" should be inserted for the word "productivity" in every news article. With this change, a business page story would read, "Canadian industry must increase the suffering of its employees at least 12 percent this year."[22]

IN THE EARLY 1990s BEV CANN, a nurse at the MFL Occupational Health Centre, told me I really ought to sit in on a presentation that Gerry Adolphe, a young meatpacking worker, was giving at that spring's health and safety conference. Working with Cann and an occupational health nurse employed by Schneider's, Adolphe was doing a detailed survey of the jobs carried out in the plant. The presentation, a mix of Adolphe's work history and his survey results, was a fascinating introduction to the world of the killing floor.

In the 1980s, when he was a leaf lard puller for Schneider's Winnipeg hog-processing plant (a job that involves tearing the fat out of the inside of hog carcasses), Adolphe began to experience a variety of repetitive strain injuries. The twisting motion left him with searing pains in his elbows. After he brought in government inspectors, a measure of job rotation was introduced. But in a small factory there are only so many jobs. And all of them are repetitive. "I was finding the problems with my elbows still are not going away and the repetitive motion of stamping and cutting is not allowing my elbows enough recovery time," he said.

Adolphe became active in the local health and safety committee and soon plunged himself into the world of ergonomics. This is the science of attempting to fit work to the worker, rather than the other way round. He began conducting a detailed survey of the jobs carried out in the plant. Adolphe's survey asked workers to break their jobs down into their component activities. This sort of breakdown reveals what it means, for example, to be a neck bone remover. In just 9.5 seconds that worker takes a twelve-pound hog shoulder from a conveyor, removes the neck bone and places the shoulder back on the conveyor. The worker then has 3.8 seconds to "recover"—but during this time the worker must maintain the edge on his knife and sterilize the blade.

There was also a detailed symptom survey that examined how a worker's tasks might be affecting his or her health. The company did make some use of his studies, which took him dozens of hours to complete, to modify a number of jobs. However, the studies had their biggest impact in a number of workers' compensation cases where the Manitoba Workers' Compensation Board was reluctant to accept a claim from a Schneider's worker with a repetitive strain. The workers were able to use Adolphe's job surveys to demonstrate the link between what they were doing and the injuries they were suffering.

The surveys also raised awareness among Schneider's workers about the potential links between their work and their health. As a result, Adolphe said people were more comfortable in coming forward with health complaints. But progress was slow and the survey consumed much of Adolphe's spare time. And when it came time to make big changes, it was clear that Schneider's had no interest in what workers had to say about working conditions.

In the mid-1990s Schneider's decided to open what it referred to as a "state-of-the-art" plant in Winnipeg. In terms of occupational health and safety, the crucial decisions are made before the first worker punches in for the first shift. Most injuries arise from the tools that are to be used, the product that is created, or the process that is employed to use those tools to create that product. And the people who decide what will be made and how it will be made are not going to have their personal health affected by their decisions. The workers, who run all the risk, have no input into these decisions. When a company such as Schneider's decides to close one plant and open another in the same city, the opportunity exists to allow workers, particularly those on the joint health-and-safety committee, to actually design the work process. Given that members of the Schneider's health and safety committee had shown such interest in ergonomics it would have been a perfect example of enlightened management. It didn't happen. As Adolphe describes it:

> The company really likes to handle all health and safety concerns on their own. They just sort of forgot our committee when we left [the old plant on] Marion Street. I was really disappointed about that and I did make that point at a labour management meeting. They did apologize and promise that we were going to work together in the future, and to a certain degree they have done that. I am very happy with the progress that we have made.

Adolphe is quite justifiably proud of what he had accomplished at Schneider's. He recognizes that even though Schneider's did not allow his committee to play a larger role in plant design, the company has put considerable attention and resources into designing the job. But he and his co-workers have a hard time believing Schneider's company officials when they say that employers are working smarter, not harder:

> We do not believe we are working smarter. We don't have time to catch our breath any more. We are going so fast, working so hard, once you start work you cannot even scratch your nose. You don't have a second to lift your hand up to scratch your nose; the product is just whizzing by you that fast.

These days Adolphe is "a belly patch guy." Working with an electric wizard knife, the makes a small cut out of the belly of passing hog carcasses. The wizard knives are modern marvels. Allegedly over $1 million was spent designing a knife that does this work with next to no vibration. But the faster the knife, the more frequent the repetition. When I spoke with Adolphe in the summer of 1998, he said that four of his co-workers had recently gone off on compensation. "Two of them have just had surgery on their hands to correct problems with their fingers, their knuckles and their wrists. So, what do you have to do? You cannot design a knife that is going to prevent an injury at that speed. It is not possible."

The issue in the packing industry, Adolphe stresses, is speed. The old Schneider's plant processed just over 250 hogs an hour. The new plant was handling 795 hogs an hour, and planned to move it up to one thousand hogs by the beginning of 1999. Adolphe says the outcome will be more injuries and more suffering:

> What the company is doing is increasing the speed and therefore the repetitive nature of all work. So you are not going to hurt yourself as quickly as you used to, it is just going to take a little longer. And if you implement job rotation, that is a good thing. But again, instead of injuring a few workers, you are injuring more workers over a longer period of time. You are just sharing the pain. There is a lot of it.

For many workers the goal is to manage their pain. "We have one line at work, there are so many people in pain, we call it the Ibuprofen line [after the name of a painkiller that many of the workers are taking]." Other workers learn what exercises to do in the morning and how to avoid aggravating their existing problems. "But unfortunately, a lot of people turn to drugs, illegal as well as the over-the-counter ones, and weekends are a time for drinking. It affects your family life, and once you get that kind of problem, you are really in a lot of trouble." And some workers have to undergo surgery to relieve carpal tunnel syndrome. To Adolphe, this is ergonomics in reverse. "We are now modifying workers to do this work. It is a very sad situation. This carpal tunnel surgery can't be good in the long term for people. It is just unbelievable in this day and age that we have to do that."

What can the joint health-and-safety committee do about line speed? Next to nothing.

> We tell them, we are going way too fast. You get the shoulders shrugged, and are told, "Sorry, there not anything we can do about

it. It just has to be done. Production levels are set and if we don't get those production levels up, we are going to go broke. Our competitor is going to take over and sell our pork to Japan, and Mexico and Russia and the United States and wherever our product is going in the international market. We are going to lose if we don't get that speed up." It seems like a race. Everybody in this industry is racing with each other, to get the most product out in the shortest time.

The production rates are not even set in Winnipeg. As a result, the workers on the health and safety committee do not bring the issue up on a regular basis. When Gerry Adolphe told me this, I asked, hesitantly, if this meant that when it came to the major health and safety issue in a high-tech, brand new plant, the committee had not been able to do anything. He was quite straightforward in his answer:

> Yeah, I would say that we are not every effective. We get a lot of little things done. We have plant tours, we talk to all the people in the work areas and if some little modification needs to be done, there is no problem there. The maintenance department is informed and the work is done. That is what our safety committee does best. We can talk about job rotation, different ways of doing the work, there is no problem there.

But he says, "Those production levels are set in Kitchener and there is nothing on this earth that is going to make them slow down for health and safety reasons or for any other reason."

The Schneider's story underscores the fact that just as they did over one hundred years ago, workers have to put their health up for sale every time they go to work. And today the bidding takes place in an international market. The right to health and safety is not inalienable under this system. It is a chopped-up right, one that can be sold. One that in fact is sold every day. At the same time committees can function, can seem to be successful, and yet fail to address the very issues that generate pain and suffering. In this way the right to participate has not provided workers with power—instead it has thrown a veil over their very powerlessness.

4

THE RIGHT TO KNOW AND THE RIGHT TO REFUSE

BOB SASS SUBVERTED THE OLD adage that knowledge is power when he reminded workers that power is power. In other words, even when workers and employers have the same knowledge about the risks of a product or process, the power relationship determines whether or not that knowledge is transferred into action. That is the central flaw with the right to participate. It has not changed the balance of power in the workplace. But what is the legacy of the other two rights: the right to know about the health hazards associated with one's job, and the right to refuse? It is hard to argue that the right to refuse is not an improvement over the previous system, where workers were obliged to do as they were told, and maybe—if they belonged to a union— file a grievance after the fact. The work refusals at Westinghouse, de Havilland and McDonnell Douglas put real pressure on the employer to change practices, and to change them quickly. The fact that workers could undertake them without fear of reprisal has to be seen as an extension of the realm of freedom on the job. And if knowledge is not necessarily power, ignorance can still be deadly. For this reason, the Workplace Hazardous Materials Information System and the training that accompanied it represented a real improvement. When Len Wheeler worked for CN in the 1970s workers were convinced that a paint they were using was making them ill. "So we went to take a look, and there were no labels. And you really had to fight long and hard to get any sort of information. So when they

78

introduced WHMIS you did not have that anymore. Material safety data sheets have to be there under law. You can get information on what you are working with." This improvement has meant that it is much more difficult to keep workers in the dark about workplace hazards. And anyone who does not believe that this has been a problem in the past might reflect upon the fate of a group of Sarnia insulation workers.

They Killed Us Too

"All that there, floating in the air, that's asbestos. That's what killed him." With a shaking finger Ralph Crevier is pointing at a photograph of his brother, Bert. In the picture a happy-looking Bert is rolling insulation around a pipe. The whole scene is flecked white with what looks like big fluffy snow flakes. The flakes are, in fact, asbestos fibres.

Crevier pauses. It is quiet in the small wood frame house that his father built in Point Edward, a working-class community on the northern edge of Sarnia, Ontario. "I lost two brothers there. My brother Bert and my brother Bev."

"There" is the Holmes Foundry Caposite Plant. All four Crevier brothers worked in the plant that produced insulated pipe and other industrial product from 1956 to 1974: Bert and Bev are dead. "They died of asbestos. Their stomachs blew out and they died. My brother Jack and I, just two of us are around. For how long, I don't know."

Crevier points back to the picture. "You want a copy of this picture, you know where to go? Workers' compensation office. They got dozens. Every time someone is having trouble getting compensation from working at the Caposite Plant, I give 'em a copy of this picture. Then Compo don't give 'em no trouble."

The Crevier boys' father had worked at Holmes Foundry before them. But he died of a heart attack in the late forties. Ralph says he thinks it was working in the factory that really killed him. After the father's death, company president Louis G. Blunt visited their mother. "He said when we get of age, they will take us in. So they killed us too, you might as well say. They killed my dad and now they turned around and killed us too."

Until it closed in 1989 the Holmes Foundry had a local reputation as dirty, dangerous place to work. The company had three divisions, all operating on one site at the edge of Sarnia. There was the Holmes Foundry Division, the Holmes Insulation Division, and the Caposite Division. The Caposite Division may well turn out to be the Westray of occupational disease. Over fifty people have died from diseases they contracted while working there. According to Jim Brophy, the director of the Occupational Health Clinic for Ontario Workers in Windsor, the numbers could eventually run into the hundreds. And as a study Brophy completed for the Canadian Autoworkers makes clear, the government was aware of the problems at Holmes Foundry since the late 1950s. "This is not just an occupational health disaster, this is a political scandal. People are dying because the government chose not to act on what it knew."

Established in 1918 to supply parts for the auto industry, the foundry was dirty and unsanitary from the outset. There was no ventilation, no showers, no sanitary toilets and no lunchroom. In 1937 a Sarnia union organizer said men were paying weekly doctor's bills to keep themselves fit to work. Many of the workers were recent immigrants from Eastern Europe who lived in shacks provided by the company. Those suspected of being pro-union were fired. Despite this intimidation, in 1937 many Holmes workers joined the Congress of Industrial Organizations. The plant manager refused to negotiate with them over their demands for toilets, showers, and a first-aid room with an attendant. Inspired by the success that sit-down strikes had enjoyed in the U.S., the unionists occupied the plant.

Playing on racial fears and anxieties, the plant managers organized a mob of three hundred Sarnia residents who attacked the foundry on March 6, 1937. To cries of "Wop" and "Hunky," the strikers were dragged from the building and beaten. One suffered a fractured spine and pelvis, and another required brain surgery after his skull was cracked. In all twenty strikers were hospitalized. Local police stood by and watched, waiting until after the strikers had been beaten before arresting them. Over sixty union members were convicted of trespass. In passing sentence, the judge told the strikers that they were foolish and stupid: "you people who come from various parts of the world will have to learn to live according to our laws." Needless to say the workers lost their jobs and were evicted from their homes.[1]

In retrospect, they may have been the lucky ones. The foundry's business boomed during the war, but the owners were reluctant to invest any money in health and safety. Frances Huggett started working at the Holmes Foundry in 1942, retiring in 1982. Suffering from emphysema, he lives with his daughter and her family in Sarnia. Years of foundry work have left him nearly deaf. His breath is short and he says he cannot lift anything. But his memory of the Holmes Foundry of 1942 is crystal clear. "That plant was a dirty, filthy plant. It was hell in that plant. Strictly hell. You could hardly see when you walked through the door lots of times." When he started at the Foundry there was no safety equipment other than safety glasses. Eventually the men were supplied with masks, but Huggett says they were useless. "The dust went right through the masks. You could not keep it out."

Like Ralph Crevier, Huggett's family has been devastated. His brother John worked with the Creviers in the Caposite operation. He died a few years ago from cancer, as did Huggett's nephew Donald. Huggett not only worked in the foundry, he lived across the street from it. He says that the air around the factory was so dirty it was impossible to dry clothes outside. Dishes had to be washed before and after each meal. "When I started there was no showers, no nothing, you had to go home and take a bath. Lots of times I would take a bath, and I would have to get out and let the water out and get back in the bath again. When you get out you start sweating a little and the dirt is still running out of you. Oh, you just could not get away from it." Huggett believes that his wife's death from cancer was the result of living with a foundry worker right next door to a foundry.

The Holmes operation turned into a slaughterhouse in 1956 when the company opened up its Caposite Insulation operation. Housed in a building next to the foundry, Caposite made insulated pipe and products, much of it used in Sarnia's chemical industry. The main insulating material was amosite asbestos. While the United Auto Workers had organized the Holmes Foundry in the 1940s, Holmes management fought and won an aggressive battle to keep the Caposite plant union free.

Asbestos is so dangerous it has had a disease named after it: asbestosis. Asbestos fibres are tiny and indestructible. When workers breathe the fibres into their lungs, they stay there. If they don't cause the deadly cancer known as mesothelioma, they scar the lungs, leaving the worker with a disabling and often fatal case of asbestosis. Today many in the health and safety community believe the product should be banned because it has no safe exposure level. This was not a mineral that should have been used under the supervision of people who had as cavalier an attitude to health as the people who ran the Holmes Foundry.

While suspicions about the health and safety risks associated with asbestos go back centuries, it was not until the early 1960s, when Dr. Irving Selikoff stumbled onto the asbestos story that the public began to fully understand the dangers this so-called miracle rock presented. A family doctor in a New Jersey working-class community, Selikoff became alarmed when he discovered that fifteen of his patients were succumbing to what should have been a rare lung disorder. All the men worked with asbestos in the same plant. Selikoff pursued this lead and eventually established the link between asbestos, cancer and mesothelioma. But in one sense his work was unnecessary. Corporations and governments had known about these hazards for years. Since 1918 U.S. insurance companies refused to sell life insurance to people who worked with asbestos. Much like the tobacco industry in the 1970s, the asbestos industry funded research throughout the 1940s and 1950s that downplayed the possible link between their product and disease.

It was at the Caposite plant that government inspectors encountered what they thought were not only the highest asbestos levels "ever encountered by this Branch in any of the plants in Ontario," but what were "probably the highest asbestos fibre concentration ever recorded."[2] It was to this plant that, one by one, the Crevier brothers were recruited when they came of age. In 1958 Ralph Crevier started at Caposite. He and his co-workers were swimming in asbestos. "You couldn't even see about three feet in front of you." At night he was in charge of cleaning the plant, blowing the asbestos away with an air hose. "On top of your hair, it used to be pure white, you would think you were going white. It used to be like cotton candy, used to fly around in the air."

The year that Ralph Crevier started at Holmes, government inspectors discovered that the asbestos levels in the Caposite Plant were twenty-eight times above the existing standard (or 6,720 times above the 2000 standard). But the government issued no improvement orders, and it was another nine years before inspectors returned. When they did it was to discover that the asbestos was still not being controlled. Only five of thirty-four samples were below the legal limit, and the average sample was 1,890 times higher than the current limit. The government issued a number of orders, none of which were enforced. When the inspectors returned five years later, in 1972, at least three cases of asbestosis had surfaced among the workers.

By then no one in government or industry could claim not to know about the dangers that the Caposite workers were facing. In 1973 *The New Yorker* magazine had run an award-winning series of reports by Paul Brodeur on the ways in which the asbestos and insulation industries had destroyed their employees' health. At the heart of his reports was the story of a plant in Tyler, Texas that had closed in the wake of studies by the U.S. National Institute of Occupational Safety and Health. What did the Pittsburgh Corning Corporation do with the asbestos that it could no longer use? Sold it to the Holmes Foundry.

According to ministry of labour documents obtained by the CAW, during the early 1970s, ministry inspectors were appalled by the conditions at Holmes. They recommended that the plant be shut down unless it was cleaned up. They also said the government had "not been as strict as we should be."[3] Time after time inspectors would issue orders only to discover the company had failed to comply. In early 1973 a clearly alarmed inspector reported that one reading in the Caposite plant was "the highest asbestos fibre concentration ever recorded." A frustrated inspector wrote, "It is my opinion that my (management) contact is more concerned with production than safety of the workers; his attitude may change."[4]

In 1972 government inspector G.S. Rajhans wrote,

"The men engaged in breaking the fibres [were] practically covered with the loose fibres. An approved type respirator is provided to this man. However, it is my contention that this respirator would not prove to be very effective in such an excessive asbestos exposure. In fact, I would not be surprised if the man develops asbestosis before too long."[5]

Finally, the government ordered that production cease. But the company simply ignored the order. No legal action was ever taken against the owners of the Holmes Foundry for exposing the workers to this deadly product at levels that exceeded existing standards. For decades the government inspectors chose friendly persuasion over prosecution. The fact that they seemed to be well aware that their approach was an ongoing and dismal failure suggests that it reflected official government policy, rather than personal sloth on their part. The fact that Sarnia was and is the chemical industry capital of Canada leaves another question hanging in the air—how many other chemical companies got a free ride from the department of labour? One also has to ask why the family doctors that treated these workers did not raise any public alarms about this disaster in the making. It is hard not to conclude that in a company town all doctors become company doctors.

The Blunt family owned the Holmes Foundry into the 1960s. Over a period of time, the family sold the firm to American Motors and by 1973 AMC owned the company outright. AMC was only interested in the foundry portion of the operation, which still produced automobile parts. In 1974 it closed the Caposite plant.

Inspectors may have heaved a sigh of relief that the Caposite operation was no longer in business, but, despite the fact that at least three cases of asbestosis had been identified, no coordinated public health measures were taken to warn the workers that they were, quite literally, walking time bombs. They had to find out the truth the hard way.

Crevier and his friends and family became increasingly aware of the Caposite plant's deadly legacy. Crevier came to call asbestos and the other diseases associated with asbestosis the African Flu because the asbestos came from South Africa. "If you get it you die. There is no cure. Nothing." Every ex-Holmes employee says the same thing: "You could not pick up the paper without reading of the death of another former Holmes foundry worker." Crevier said, "There used to be 150 people working in the Caposite building. I bet only ten of them are still alive."

But, like the asbestos that used to fill the air in the Caposite Plant, the Holmes Foundry scandal might have simply drifted along and settled between the cracks if it were not for the efforts of Bob Clarke. A long-time Holmes worker, Clarke served through the 1980s as the United Auto Workers, and later Canadian Auto Workers, plant chairman. In that job he fought an ongoing battle to clean up the main foundry and he assisted former Holmes workers in their fights for compensation. Steve Nield chaired the union's health and safety committee in the late 1980s at Holmes. He remembers Clarke as a man who never said no to a worker. "And he never stopped fighting on health and safety issues. It did not matter who you were and what you had done. He had unbelievable compassion for his members at Holmes Foundry."

Many of the fifty-one occupational disease claims from the Holmes Foundry that have been recognized by the Ontario Workers' Compensation Board (now the Workers Safety and Insurance Board) were won with Clarke's assistance. After the entire Holmes operation closed in 1991 workers continued to be struck down by occupational disease.

The Ontario government knew all about the elevated death rates among Holmes workers. A 1987 study done by the Ontario ministry of labour found a six-fold increase in lung cancer mortality among the Holmes workers exposed to asbestos for two years or more. There was an eleven-fold increase in respiratory disease mortality and a four-fold excess of all malignancies. The study also identified five cases of mesothelioma among former Holmes workers. Three of the five workers died at less than fifty years of age and all were less than sixty years old.

But it was still up to the individual workers to go out and fight their own case for compensation. And despite the fact that workers who are claiming compensation for industrial diseases have the deck stacked against them, the Holmes workers and their families have been very successful. Of fifty-four claims that have been put forward at Holmes, fifty-one had been accepted by 1999. Jim Brophy says no other workplace has ever had anywhere near that percentage of disease claims accepted. The numbers do not reflect the compassion of the compensation system, but rather Bob Clarke's hard work and the murderous conditions at Holmes.

In 1998 Clarke contacted the Windsor Occupational Health Clinic for support. He also started to attract media attention to the issue. Steve Nield, who is now a workplace health and safety inspector, remembers being in the kitchen of his house when he heard the Holmes foundry mentioned in a television newscast.

> I ran into the living room. And outside the meeting hall they were interviewing this gentleman, and he was talking about the atroci-ties of Holmes Foundry. I did not recognize him. It was not until they flashed his name on the bottom of the screen that I recog-nized that it was Bob Clarke. Here was a guy that was probably pushing around 250 pounds—a jolly rotund guy. I bet you he weighed less than a hundred pounds. The visualization of him was very disturbing. That was the standout moment when I realized the devastating impact of Holmes Foundry had had.

Clarke had come down with cancer.

Working with the CAW, the clinic held a public meeting for former Holmes employees in September 1998. It was a heart-rending day. Over three hundred people showed up. The staff was overwhelmed, physically and emotionally. Jim Brophy clearly recalls the moment. "Two brothers came, holding each others' hands. Both in their sixties, both of them with cancer. Many of these workers had been refugees after the Second World War, from Eastern Europe. They came and worked in these jobs because that was the only way they could survive. Some of them still spoke broken English. They needed their children to translate for them." The wife of a plant engineer had mesothelioma, a disease she likely contracted from her husband's clothes. Another woman's husband had actually appeared in adver-tisements promoting Holmes' products. This woman too had mesothelioma, a disease her husband had brought home with his paycheque.

Nield recalls being moved by the sight of men who were once big strong foundry workers now small and frail, chained to their oxygen supply. Nield was able to renew many old acquaintances, but there was a big hole at the meeting. Bob Clarke, "the man who *was* Holmes Foundry as far as the workers were concerned," was not there. He had just been moved into palliative care. He died at the end of October, 1998. Said Nield, "Once he contracted cancer he went down fast. That's what has happened in all the cases where anybody has come down with any types of cancers that worked at Holmes Foundry."

As a result of the clinic hundreds of new files were opened. For the first time someone began talking to the Holmes workers as a group about the conditions they experienced: something that for eighty years the Sarnia medical establishment, the Ontario government, and Holmes Foundry management never did.

The Caposite plant is still a health threat. When the plant closed in the 1974, a government inspector wrote that "there is likely to be a considerable amount of asbestos dust in the fabric of the building and on the steelwork."[6] It is extraordinarily difficult and expensive to remove asbestos that has been properly installed. Asbestos that was blown throughout a plant with air hoses for decades and allowed to settle in every nook and cranny is all but impossible to remove.

The Right to Know What?

THE HOLMES FOUNDRY SCANDAL is still only coming to light. Because the plant is no longer in operation and because asbestos is no longer used as an insulating product, there is a danger that people may view this as a tragic story from our industrial past. Others might argue that under the internal responsibility system workers would have far more access to information and more power to act on that information than the Holmes workers enjoyed. There could be no bigger mistake.

The men who worked in the Caposite plant were working with a product that both the employer and the government knew to be dangerous. They were being exposed to it at levels that exceeded government regulations. And those regulations were far too loose to protect their health. Workers may not be exposed to asbestos any more in the Holmes Foundry, but right across this country Canadian workers are being exposed to many cancer-causing materials, and the exposures are often far above safe levels.

Machine shop workers, for example, are regularly exposed to cutting fluids, sometimes called mineral oils. These fluids are a complex mixture of chemicals, usually derived from shale or petroleum. They are used for a variety of purposes, including cooling metal when it is being molded or cut. In many machine shops it hangs in the air as a fine mist. Since the 1940s it has been known that British textile workers who were exposed to these fluids had excess rates of skin cancer. The Ontario compensation regulations specifically recognized mineral oil exposure as a cause of skin cancer. But it was not until the late 1990s that the full extent of the dangers of mineral oils and cutting fluids began to be publicly recognized.

In the mid-1980s General Motors, acting under union pressure, contracted Harvard University researchers to conduct a study of 46,000 Michigan autoworkers. They found excess cancer in the larynx, esophagus, colon, rectum, and stomach. Little of this information was made public. It has taken a death and a union campaign, not employer or government action, to draw attention to the dangers of cutting fluids.

In the summer of 1996 Bud Jimmerfield, the president of a small CAW Local in Amherstburg, Ontario, got in contact with the Windsor clinic. Jimmerfield had worked for SKD Corporation, an auto parts company in Amherstburg, from 1966 until the plant closed in 1997. He was no stranger to health and safety issues, having served as the chairperson of the plant's health and safety committee for over a decade. He became a health and safety activist following a fatal accidents in the plant. He was well known at the clinic, having helped out in a study of the health hazards of autoworkers in the Amherstburg area. But this time he was not contacting the clinic in his role as an activist. He was a patient, having just been diagnosed with esophageal cancer. He was forty-eight years old and had eight children.

He died in January 1998 following a harrowing battle with the disease, which had spread throughout his body. In the fall of that year, his family, with the support of the CAW, scored a landmark workers' compensation victory. Using the recently uncovered data on cutting fluids they won compensation based on a claim that Jimmerfield's death was due to his years of exposure to cutting fluids.

As in the case of Bob Clarke, the cancer took a tremendous toll on Jimmerfield's body. Jim Brophy recalls that Jimmerfield went from being a 220-pound union activist to looking like a human skeleton. He lost his hair, he was constantly nauseous, and was in constant pain. "In spite of all of that he continued to go out and speak publicly about this issue."

The Bud Jimmerfield story is the asbestos story all over again. Industry was aware of the hazards long before workers knew about them. Government was aware. Workers continued to be exposed. And this took place despite the existence of the right-to-know laws. Jimmerfield said that he was completely unaware of the dangers of the cutting fluids he worked with for thirty years, even though he was a health and safety activist who actually led courses on how workers should use the WHMIS laws. Jimmerfield came to see that the rights that he had sought to enforce and to encourage other workers to use had failed him.

Workers exposed at levels ten times below the current legal limit will still bear an excess cancer and respiratory disease risk. Despite this, the Ontario government has still not lowered the exposure levels for workers exposed to metal working fluids. The CAW has actually started negotiating lower exposure levels into its collective agreements. It is a move that, as Cathy Walker says, indicates just how seriously the union takes this issue. It also indicates very plainly the fact that worker health and safety is just another chip on the bargaining table. CAW member Ken Bondy is proud of the job his union had done in improving protection for its members. But he recognizes that members have been forced to put their health on the bargaining table. "Unfortunately, in today's global economics our health is for sale. We have to do the best job possible to ensure that we are not going to be sold out, that we are not going to get caught up in a race to the bottom and look at the possible sacrificing of people's health or lives simply to keep your job."

The cutting fluid story is a reminder that WHMIS data sheets are far from complete. What has been left off can be of greater importance than what is on them. Asbestos and cutting fluids are just two examples of cases where corporations kept quiet about health hazards. It would be astonishing if these were the only two examples. And if a chemical has not been fully tested—and most have not— then the information that workers are in greatest need of may not exist.

Women's Work: The Great Unknown

THE RIGHT TO KNOW IS NOT only limited when governments and corporations keep silent about dangers they have discovered in the workplace. The right to know does not do a worker any good if no one has bothered to investigate whether a job or task is dangerous in the first place. And it is often the case that the jobs that go unexamined are the jobs that are held by women.

The most investigated jobs and hazards are the ones that are linked to traumatic injuries. Everyone agrees that mining, logging, and construction work are dangerous. While one might argue about how well enforced or appropriate they are, the law sets out specific guidelines for these industries. Men traditionally hold the bulk of the jobs in these dangerous industries. In fact, it is no secret that in Canada, and indeed, around the world, there are clear divisions between what is considered men's work and women's work. It is difficult to make many generalizations about the differences between men's jobs and women's jobs other than the fact that men's work tends to be much better paid. Men's work can require considerable strength and may entail considerable risk, but not all men are miners or loggers. And men's work can allow them more autonomy and control over what they do—there are still more male executives than secretaries, for example. However, there are also many many more male assembly line workers than executives.

These sorts of comparisons mask as much as they reveal. For the supposedly light work that women do has real physical components. The kindergarten teacher spends her day stooped over her students' desks. The seamstress must perform a limited range of motions over and over again, all the while keeping her attention focussed on the detailed work she is doing. The Canadian grocery store clerk—unlike her French counterpart—spends her working day standing up, performing repetitive actions. The people performing these jobs rarely lose a limb at work. Nor are they likely to come down with mesothelioma (unless their office has been insulated with asbestos). From the point of view of the health and safety system, they are out of sight and out of mind. The invisibility of the many health risks that women may face lead Montreal researcher Karen Messing to title her book on women and occupational health *One-Eyed Science*.

Messing is a professor of biological science at the University of Quebec in Montreal and the former director of the Centre for the Study of Biological Interactions in Environmental Health or CINBIOSE as it is known in Quebec. Because she lectures nationally and internationally on issues of women's occupational health hazards she has often found herself in the situation where people expressed bewilderment at what she was going to talk about—after all, women's work is safe. She has a standard response:

I am interested in people who are suffering. There are people suffering who are miners and there are people suffering who are telephone operators or sewing machine operators or bank tellers. A lot more effort right now is being devoted to the miner than to the vast majority of women workers. I think some effort should be devoted to the psychological and physical suffering that is undergone by these women.

Sewing machine operators for example may do close to two thousand motions a day. This is extremely painful after a while and can be very tiring and has been shown that it leads to disability at an older age. Bank tellers ... stand all day. In North America we think tellers should be standing so as to give an impression that they are available to be consulted at all times. This prolonged standing is associated with a lot of pain in the legs and lower back.

This is real suffering, to my mind unnecessary suffering, and something should be done about it.

But little will be done unless these jobs are studied. Messing points out that most scientists are men and have little connection with the daily lives of most working people. Indeed, her involvement in health and safety arose in large measure out of a unique agreement between CINBIOSE and the Quebec union movement to have the university assist unions with research projects. In the first project that Messing was involved in, the union wanted to know more about the effect of radiation on human genes. "What I thought were rather abstract questions about physical effects of ions on molecules turned out to be quite meaningful for people's lives. I found out some fairly horrible things about what was happening quite close by me that I had been unaware of in terms of people being exposed to radioactive dusts or exposed to chemicals that really hurt them."

But, as Messing points out, most women workers are not so lucky. She uses the case of restaurant waitresses to illustrate why no one is looking into the health problems many working women face. According to Messing there have been no studies conducted on the health and safety risks run by waitresses. "Waitresses are workers whom everyone is exposed to. They see waitresses running around carrying heavy trays. I was a waitress myself, so I know about the problems like sore feet, sore legs and sore back." But the odds are against there ever being a study into the health hazards of waiting on tables. First of all waitresses are caught in a Catch-22 situation. Most of them find the work so hard that they usually leave it after just a few months. And they rarely file claims for workers' compensation. As long as they are not filing for compensation, governments and academics are likely to take the position that they have no problems. And as long as there are other young women prepared to take a job as a waitress, restaurant owners are unlikely to improve working conditions.

An application to fund a study examining the health hazards that waitresses face would be turned down because there are no known health hazards to waiting on tables: after all, waitresses don't collect workers' compensation in large numbers. But as long as there are no studies into the job, it is difficult to see how a worker would ever win a compensation case for long-term injuries sustained from waiting on tables. "I can remember when we asked for money to do research on a particular chemical and to discover its effect on reproduction," Messing recalls. "We were told that the money would not be forthcoming because there was no evidence that existed that showed that this would be a problem. To get the money, there has to be some evidence that there is a problem to study."

Funding agencies would also raise questions about the scientific possibility of doing a study on waitresses. It might be necessary to study five hundred workers for a year or so, but waitressing has such a high turnover rate that the initial number of people to be studied may well have to be much higher or the study would have no statistical significance. In other words the fact that waiting on tables is a low-paid, high-turnover job militates against anyone studying its health and safety risks. Needless to say this applies to many other service sector jobs in which women are employed.

Another objection would be that the problems waitresses encounter are not true illnesses. Chronic pain and suffering are neither broken bones nor diseased lungs—and in the minds of many experts they should simply be tolerated. So waitresses remain unstudied. And if they try to exercise their right to know or to discover the hazards of standing for eight hours a day, of lifting certain types of trays, or of shift work in the food services industry, they will draw a blank.

This neglect extends far beyond the problems faced by waitresses. Women's work is far less studied than men's work—and women are omitted from more than studies into the aches and pains of the service industry. According to Messing, women were only considered as a separate variable in 14 percent of the papers written on occupational cancer between 1980 and 1993. "This was not done because people want to hurt women, but because people did not think of hairdressers or laboratory technicians as chemical workers."

Messing once submitted a proposal to study the health issues faced by women entering non-traditional manual jobs. The study was intended to see if jobs that had been designed for the average man might create muscle and bone problems for the average women. The funding agency recommended that Messing and her colleagues amend their application so that it simply proposed looking at the problems faced by people working with tools that were poorly designed for their physiology. They agreed, reluctantly. The proposal was approved, but the portion of the research that would have studied women in non-traditional jobs was not funded. It was not a priority issue. And at that rate never will be.

Educate and Agitate

THE REFORMS OF THE MID-1970S sought to give workers greater access to available scientific knowledge. But it was also hoped that the changes would generate a greater respect for worker knowledge as well. This is not a knowledge that comes from the laboratory or the questionnaire, but from lived experience—what Bob Sass calls "knowledge from their bodies."

The growing role of the expert, which has been aided rather than held in check by the right to know, has in Sass's opinion lopped off workers' experience. "Their experiences and how they made sense of the workplace became irrelevant in the operation of these committees in practice." Technical knowledge is not unimportant. In the case of some health hazards it is crucial—when decades can elapse between an exposure and the onset of a disease, technical expertise can be a lifesaver. But on its own technical knowledge never cleaned up a workplace.

When one reads the history of the health and safety movement, one is struck by the fact that so many stories have their starting point in a conversation that a group of workers had one day over lunch about their health problems. George Smith, the Saskatchewan gas instrument technician whose battle for compensation was such a learning experience for Bob Sass, began to link his health problems to his job after discovering that his co-workers were suffering from the same symptoms he had. In the 1980s workers at a Winnipeg bus plant wondered about the potential health effects of working with cadmium. At a local meeting, the president looked up the metal's potential side effects in a handy question and answer book published by the union. Before he was through the list, he put the book down and exclaimed, "My god, I don't believe it." He had just catalogued the symptoms that the women in the company's soldering department had been complaining of. This marriage of expertise and experience was the launching pad for much of the health and safety activism of the 1980s.

But along the way the emphasis on worker experience and activism was lost. Many of the health and safety acts passed in the 1970s required that members of the newly created workplace health and safety committees be given time off work for training. Initially, the training focused on the content of the laws and common hazards. The amount of training available has increased over the years, although it is far from clear that employers always ensure that workers get the training they are mandated to receive. In some provinces this training is provided through private companies or by government-sanctioned joint employer-employee training programs. As a satisfied business executive noted, this sort of training has served to de-politicize health and safety.

Bob DeMatteo was the Ontario Public Service Employees Union health and safety director during the 1980 and 1990s. It was a period marked by a joint (or bipartite) management and labour approach to training. It was an approach that he feels took the wind out of the labour movement's sails. Where originally training had been what he calls "activist training" that stressed the importance of organizing and educating the membership to provide health and safety activists with a power basis, it became technical training. "And frankly what I think we are doing is training workers to death—literally speaking. We are not providing them with the kind of protections that are needed." At the same time DeMatteo worries that occupational health and safety training has become too technical:

> We have to train our people, not to become technical experts, because that is what we have done and that has been a serious mistake. We have got to train them—I don't know if this is a teachable thing—but we have got to teach them how to become trade union activists. They have to organize the workforce around this particular working condition issue, like they do with any other working condition issue that they have to mobilize around. That is what is missing right now and that is what has occurred over the years.

In response to these concerns, which were shared by many labour educators and health and safety activists, the Canadian Labour Congress has revamped its approach to health and safety education. In particular, training courses were reviewed to make sure they addressed the danger of members being co-opted by management. The focus was moving from the technical—be it legal or medical—to the political.

Access to scientific research and knowledge is invaluable. And workers should not have to wait until they start exhibiting the most serious, and often irreversible, symptoms of workplace poisoning before they realize they have a problem. But to see workplace health and safety as a technical issue, to ignore the role that power and politics play in the workplace, is to turn one's back on the real history of workplace health and safety.

The Right to Refuse

FOR MANY EMPLOYERS THE RIGHT to refuse unsafe work was the most alarming of the new worker rights introduced in the 1970s and '80s. While workers had previously enjoyed a common law right to refuse dangerous work, this right was limited. Judges and arbitrators would take into consideration the willingness of other workers to perform the task and the degree to which the risk was normal for the industry. Finally, in many cases judges could not reinstate workers who were disciplined for refusing unsafe work. Instead they could simply order their former employer to pay them wrongful dismissal damages.

When Howard Pawley's NDP government introduced the right in 1982, it met with stiff opposition from the business community. Business leaders correctly understood that this right was an affront to their legitimacy and their authority. It assumed that workers were, in certain circumstances, being asked to undertake unsafe work against their will. In a sense, it turned the workplace on its head: in the workplace employees are hired to undertake all legal activities that the employer directs them to undertake. The employer's authority may be limited by various laws or the terms of a specific employment contract, but it has traditionally been the case that the employee was expected to do as told and then make a complaint to the appropriate authorities.

The right to refuse, without fear of punishment, when the worker had a reasonable belief that the work was unsafe meant that in certain circumstances the worker was to be freed of the very obligation that made him or her a worker: the obligation to obey the employer's direction. These thoughts were foremost in the minds of Canada Packers Winnipeg production manager W.R. McGill and safety coordinator Fred Carlson when they wrote to the government in the fall of 1982. In that letter they stated:

> This is a topic to which we cannot relate. One would think that many people are injured every year as a result of being instructed to do dangerous work. This is simply not the case. What is meant by dangerous work? Certainly some jobs are more dangerous than others by their very nature. Care and diligence are required to perform them safely.

> To us this appears to be an issue which suggests that management people are universally irresponsible and have no sense of responsibility towards their employees. The facts do not bear this out. If workers have the right to refuse dangerous work then who will define what is dangerous and who will bear the consequences of abuse of this right?

> Management have a right to operate their plant productively and without stoppage. Management have a responsibility to ensure this is done without placing their employees in grave or unusual risk situations. What is the relevance of giving the power to affect operations to individuals who have no responsibilities beyond their own specific tasks.

> … As a general statement we can say that we are concerned about trends in legislation which give prerogatives to individuals and groups who have no accountability for their actions. The role of management is to manage and to accept responsibility for and remain accountable for their decisions. The reality of the workplace is that the vast majority of accidents are caused by workers failing to follow already established rules and policies.[7]

The strength of feeling expressed in this letter indicates the degree of opposition that would arise if governments were ever to give the joint health-and-safety committees the power to enforce their recommendations.

But the Canada Packers managers need not have worried. The right to refuse has not revolutionized the Canadian workplace. On a number of occasions workers have exercised this right and brought about real change. But those are the exceptions. The right to refuse is probably the right that workers are most aware of and the one that they are least likely to invoke.

The Canada Packers managers would argue that this is because for the most part workers are not being directed to perform unsafe work, and in fact, are only injured when they disobey management directives. While young *untrained* workers are at high risk, and there are of course people who do engage in risky behaviour on the job, just as they do when they are not at work, careless workers are not the cause of most accidents. As long ago as the 1920s industrial engineers came to the realization that it was a cop-out to blame injuries on careless workers. They recognized that this was simply an ideological holdover from the days when employers could use worker negligence as a part of their defence in a liability case. The most successful corporate safety campaigns were the ones that involved workers in identifying hazards and developing solutions.[8]

Nor has anyone ever suggested that on a daily basis employers are consciously ordering their employees to do work that they believe to be dangerous. But as the statistics cited at the outset of this book demonstrate, many workplaces in this country are unsafe. In 1994-95 the Manitoba Workplace Safety and Health Branch investigated sixteen deaths and issued twenty-eight stop-work orders. In addition, it ordered improvements in 1,606 instances. Yet in that year, the branch dealt with only nine cases involving the right to refuse. It should be noted that the number of improvement orders issued that year was down from 2,888 the year before, a reflection of "the changing approach of the branch. Emphasis is being placed on creating a climate to induce permanent change within the safety culture of the workplace."[9]

In many jurisdictions the spirit of the law has been watered down by changes in government policy and by court rulings. Where the right to refuse once took a worker's individual condition into account in determining whether the work was unsafe, today in some Canadian jurisdictions a lack of training is the only time the worker's individual condition can be invoked when exercising the right. (This means that if the work is judged to be safe for the average trained worker, it is safe, even if the worker suffers from certain conditions that would make the work unsafe for him or her.) Increasingly inspectors are required to determine if the worker actually has the right to refuse before determining if the work is dangerous. And if the situation is deemed to be normal for the industry, it is increasingly unlikely that the worker's use of the right will be upheld. A study done by Marc Renaud and Chantal St-Jacques indicated that under these restrictive rules only 40 percent of work refusals were viewed as being justified. However, in 40 percent of the supposedly unjustified cases, the inspectors issued improvement orders.[10] In other words, in these cases the workplace was unsafe, but the worker had no right to refuse.

Vivienne Walters has studied those cases in Ontario where workers claimed they had been disciplined for exercising their right to refuse unsafe work. She found that the Ontario Labour Relations Board was more likely to rule in a worker's favour if it concluded the worker was a satisfactory employee who was not seeking revenge. Talkative and opinionated workers did not fare as well. The board also indicated that in situations where the employer needed to take strong disciplinary actions to maintain control of the workplace, it was prepared to rule in the employer's case, even though the facts would have normally led it to rule in favour of the worker.[11]

Finally, many workers simply do not believe that the government can protect them if they refuse work. Workers told Vivienne Walters and Ted Haines that, "If you want the job, you take what you've got," and, "I'm afraid to complain too much or I may lose my job altogether."[12] Many unionized workers are leery of exercising this right— for non-unionized workers the right might as well not exist. Law professor Eric Tucker found that in 1983-84 in Ontario, 91 percent of refusals came from unionized workers.[13] It is clear that the fear of the sack puts tremendous pressure on workers not to make use of this right. Throughout the 1980s the work refusals declined as unemployment rose.[14]

The law states that workers are not to be disciplined for exercising their right to refuse. However, according to the United Steelworkers local in Thompson, Manitoba, governments are lax in prosecuting employers who do discipline workers in such situations. During the mid-1990s the Steelworkers felt that the government was taking a hands-off approach to worker discipline at Inco. On two occasions, Thompson miners were disciplined for exercising their right to refuse. The union has successfully fought these disciplinary actions through the grievance procedure. But the president of the Thompson local of the Steelworkers, Bob Desjarlais, believed the government ought to have taken legal action against the company. For its part, the company maintained management had been unaware that the workers involved were exercising a right to refuse.

The government took the position that this was an internal matter between the company and the union, one that has been resolved in the union's behalf. A frustrated Desjarlais asked, what is likely to happen if a worker who has been disciplined in the past is ordered to do something he believes to be dangerous. "He might say, 'I am not going to do it, I am not going to put my life at risk.' But what happens if he will be disciplined and possibly terminated as a result of that discipline. The union will fight for him—and he will probably get his job back. But he will have to go six or eight months without a paycheque. What is that worker going to do? He is going to go ahead and do that job. And that is a scandal."

This story from a Ford Motors plant in Windsor, Ontario provides the clearest insight into the limitations that workers face when they refuse to do dangerous work. The Canadian Auto Workers, which represents Ford workers, is one of this country's strongest and most effective unions. And it aggressively pursues health and safety issues. It is very unlikely that Ford would ever get away with dismissing a worker for refusing unsafe work. But that does not mean that they are beyond the reach of management discipline. In the 1990s

Ken Bondy was working as a repairman on a Ford assembly line. Problems on the line led a co-worker to ask him to put on the power lockout and fetch the tools needed to repair a specific problem. At the time Bondy was worried because the worker making the request was already in a dangerous position and should have previously put on the power lockout. Before he could do anything, Bondy's supervisor told him to forget the lockout: get the tools and get on with the repair. He disobeyed the directive and the next day found himself called on the carpet.

> I told the supervisor that his priorities were a little mixed up. If that worker had been crushed or killed by that piece of equipment, he would not be going home the next day. But no matter what happened to workers, tomorrow we would make another engine in that plant. It should be people's lives that are the top priority, not the product.

No formal discipline was taken against Bondy. But he was never again selected to go on what he viewed as one of the cushier jobs at Ford. "Ultimately that supervisor used his power to ensure that I did not get that job ever again. I was moved off to a more dirty, hard job on the plant."

None of this should be taken as rejecting the value of the right to refuse. It has undoubtedly saved lives. And because the right to refuse provides workers with a real measure of power in the workplace it needs to be defended. However, it is only when workers have exercised this right *en masse*, actions which the current laws rarely countenance, that they have been able to make dramatic gains in workplace health and safety.

As Bob Sass concluded, the right to know and the right to refuse have turned out to be weak rights, not strong rights. They have been undermined by economic conditions and by employer resistance. And as the statistics suggest they are responsible for, at best, modest improvements in workplace health and safety. It is a dispiriting legacy—made all the worse by the fact that this regime of workplace regulation has been used as a justification for cutting back on inspection and enforcement.

5

NO ONE WAS KILLED: THE LIMITS ON THE EXTERNAL RESPONSIBILITY SYSTEM

IN THE FALL OF 1996 MELFORD NICKOSHIE, a Winnipeg construction worker, nearly lost a leg when a trench he was digging collapsed, leaving him buried in mud to his waist. It took four hours to dig him out, by which time his leg was crushed. Not surprisingly this harrowing event was front-page news in Winnipeg. And the provincial government soon launched an investigation into Kordite Construction, the firm in charge of the project where the accident took place.

It turned out that the government was all too familiar with the company and its practices. Only a year before, Provincial Construction, a company run by the same owner, had been ordered to shut down a trench excavation because it had not been properly shored up to prevent a collapse. Government officials say that they vigorously prosecute people who violate trenching laws. But, government officials explained to the media, no charges were laid against Provincial Construction "because the company shut down and essentially disappeared."

The owner had not taken it on the lam like a wild desperado. He had simply changed company names and continued to do business, apparently in the same careless fashion. The difference between what happened in 1995 and 1996 was simple. In 1995 Provincial Construction violated the construction code, but no one was hurt. Therefore the government did not pursue the firm. In 1996 Kordite

Construction injured one of its workers, and more significantly, the injury made it on to the front page of the newspapers. Thus is revealed one of the key tenets of health and safety law: if no one is hurt, there is no prosecution.

Another event in 1996 further underlined that lesson. In January of that year construction scaffolding at the Health Sciences Centre collapsed in a windstorm. Hundreds of thousands of dollars of damage were done to the HSC, which had to temporarily close its Emergency Ward.

Prior to the collapse two union members had complained about the dangerous condition of the scaffolding. After the complaints were lodged, the company was unable to provide the government with the required architectural drawings. Following the collapse it was revealed that the company in question had not met standards at a different construction site the previous year. But none of this had led to a prosecution. Instead government inspectors—in keeping with policies laid down by their political masters—exercised their discretion and instructed the firm to comply with the law. During the ensuing, and short-lived, flurry of media attention, government officials stated that there was no proof that increased prosecutions leads to improved health and safety. At the time a construction firm representative summed up the official position neatly when he said, "I don't know why this is turning into such a big issue. No one was killed."

This hands-off approach to the enforcement of health and safety laws has been in effect ever since the first health and safety laws were written in Great Britain nearly two hundred years ago. For it was with the construction of the dark Satanic mills of the industrial revolution that societies began placing legal limits on what could be done to workers. The laws were required for a number of reasons. First of all, if factory acts were not put in place to curb the worst aspects of the industrial revolution, particularly the exploitation of children, there were fears that a revolution might break out. The industrial revolution had given rise to an organized and militant labour movement. This movement coalesced around the campaign for the People's Charter in early 1800s. The Chartists' demands today seem rather ordinary—the vote, representation by population, and the secret ballot. But these demands for a society of equals struck a chord with British workers, who turned out in hundreds of thousands at Chartist demonstrations. And this political energy put fear in the hearts of the British ruling class. It was also hoped that laws would create a level playing field, which would allow companies to survive without brutalizing their workforces. Finally, factory laws, it was thought, would take workplace health and safety out of the political field and render it a technical matter.

After prolonged controversy, the first British factory act was passed in 1833. Fines under this act ranged between one and twenty pounds, while magistrates had the option to grant a complete discharge. During these early years inspection came close to constituting an outright conspiracy between the inspectors and employers. According to historian W.G. Carson the inspectors were told to be "in communication exclusively with the employers, with the view of making the law acceptable to them."[1] The inspectors' reports emphasized the difficulties that employers would experience in adhering to the law.

A turning point in the history of inspection came when a new law limiting the employment of young people was set to come into effect. The law had been adopted during a short-lived economic boom, but was proclaimed during an economic downturn. When the law was passed it was thought that it would only affect small-scale and marginal employers, but during the depression even the largest employers were dependent on the low-wage work of youngsters. If the inspectors vigorously enforced the law they would have been laying charges against many of the nation's leading industrialists. It is doubtful the courts would have encouraged this practise. As it was, the judges, many of them factory owners themselves, imposed very low fines when they did convict. Between 1836 and 1842, 68 percent of all fines were a pound or less. Often employers were let off with no fine at all. The courts often acquitted employers because they were able to shift responsibility to a junior manager, or even the workers who, in this era of subcontracting, had hired their own children.

In the end the inspectors did not enforce the child labour provisions. Instead of using prosecution and enforcement, they were told to use persuasion to limit the practise. In 1837 one inspector wrote that he intended to delay "resort to coercive measures until all others have proved to be totally unavailing."[2]

Similar patterns prevailed in Ontario when the industrial revolution hit North America. The first factory act was adopted by the Ontario government in 1884, but only after a typically Canadian jurisdictional battle between the Liberal provincial government in Toronto and the federal Conservative government. Three inspectors were appointed to cover the entire province. Unions of the 1880s complained that there were three saloon inspectors for the City of Toronto alone, while every county had a school inspector. (This has remained a staple trade union criticism. In a May 2000 brief to the Manitoba Workers' compensation Board, Cathy Walker of the CAW pointed out that in nearly every Canadian province, "there are more game wardens than health and safety inspectors.")[3] York University legal historian Eric Tucker argues that from the outset the inspectors chose persuasion rather than prosecution as their main tool in enforcing the law. Unions noticed this and complained that inspections were really pre-arranged guided tours that rarely led to any improvements in working conditions. When inspectors did press charges it was against firms that were illegally employing minors or women. The courts were prepared to back up the inspectors: prosecutions ended in convictions and the fines were in keeping with what the inspectors recommended.

By the turn of the century each of Ontario's inspectors had well over a thousand workplaces to inspect. And according a veteran inspector, it was understood that "it was the wish of the government that the factories act shall be enforced in an efficient manner, with as little friction and annoyance as possible."[4] In their reports the inspectors made it clear that they saw themselves as educators who were attempting to teach both workers and employers how to perform their tasks in a safe manner. They argued that safety paid, and once employers understood this simple fact, many hazards would be done away with. They also believed that worker carelessness was a major cause of industrial accidents. They were not there to remake the workplace. In 1899 one of them wrote that inspectors "take the machines as they find them, excepting guarding, as far as practicable."[5]

ONE HUNDRED YEARS LATER governments are, by and large, still taking workplaces as they find them. The impact of the dead hand of past practice is quite visible when one looks at how governments regulate chemical exposures in the workplace. Across Canada governments regularly turn to the American Conference of Governmental Industrial Hygienists for guidance in determining occupational exposure levels. The ACGIH publishes a list of Threshold Limit Values. Known as TLVs, these are meant to be unofficial guides to acceptable exposure levels. In fact they have been widely adopted by the U.S., German, and British governments at various times. According to the ACGIH, "Threshold limit values refer to airborne con centrations of substances and represent conditions under which it is believed that nearly all workers may be repeatedly exposed day after day without adverse effect." The idea is that once exposure crosses the threshold it has been transformed from harmless to dangerous. However, from the outset TLVs were developed with one eye on the market—in 1948 the conference acknowledged that while it was attempting to develop thresholds that would protect workers, it did not want to place an impossible burden on the manufacturer.

Two academic critics of TLVs, S.A. Roach and S. M. Rappaport, argue that TLVs are more likely to represent the levels that industry is attaining at any given time than a threshold that divides dangerous from safe exposure levels. They point out that the ACGIH definition of TLVs contains a slippery concept from the outset. The TLVs are meant to protect "nearly all workers." Rappaport and Roach reviewed tests of the TLVs and discovered that the concept of "nearly all" in fact left quite a few workers in danger. When they looked at tests for the 1976 TLVs, Rappaport and Roach found that "[M]ost studies demonstrated an incidence of adverse effect which was substantially above zero at the TLV and which was even 100 percent in some cases (eight instances). This was particularly true regarding exposure to irritants, where 93 of 174 individuals exposed at or below the TLV experienced effects." [6]

Their review of the studies for twenty-nine substances in the 1986 TLVs concluded that, "The incidence of adverse effects at the TLV again ranged from zero (thirteen instances) to 100 percent (three instances), and ... it appeared that, overall, 14 percent of employees exposed at or below the 1986 TLV were adversely affected."[7] To put it bluntly, between one and six and one and seven workers would be adversely affected by exposures at or below the recommended TLVs. When they went through the actual studies they found cases of people—often the majority of people involved in the test—complaining of adverse reactions at levels that were well below the TLVs that were eventually adopted. Roach and Rappaport noted that it was clear from their research that more than science was involved in setting TLVs—the question is, what else? They could not help but point out that "the TLVs represent levels of exposure which were perceived by the Committee to be realistic and attainable at the time."[8] Whatever they were, Threshold Limit Values were not thresholds. These researchers were not alone in their conclusions. The West Germans reviewed the TLVs—which they had adopted in 1955—and concluded that less than ten percent rested on sufficient testing.

Two other researchers, Barry Castleman and Grace E. Ziem, have shone a searchlight on the role that corporations have played in establishing TLVs. For despite its name, the American Conference of Governmental Industrial Hygienists is not a government organization. Rather it is a voluntary professional organization—with very limited ability to carry out its own research on the substances for which it is setting standards. Since its formation in 1946 it has largely been dependent on industry for most of its data. Needless to say, there was no requirement for industry to file data with the ACGIH, and they didn't. In the 1960s the head of the ACGIH regularly complained about the lack of data the conference received from industry.

This situation changed in the 1970s when, following the passage of the Occupational Safety and Health Act in the United States, the federal government began to use TLVs as legal standards. Full-time employees of chemical companies became much more involved and influential in the setting of TLVs. The Dow Chemical Company in particular was well represented on committees involved in establishing TLVs. According to Castleman and Ziem, 104 of the six hundred TLVs developed in 1986 were based largely on unpublished corporate communication. And when they attempted to get copies of these corporate documents, they were for the most part not available. In 1980 Dr. Hector Blejer resigned from the TLV Committee, protesting what he saw as "an increasingly strong pro-industry bias ... particularly almost all the Committee consultants and among the members who consult privately for private industry."[9] From 1970 to 1988 corporate representatives took the lead in establishing the TLVs for over 100 substances—thirty-six of which were carcinogens.[10]

According Castleman and Ziem, the ACGIH has never attempted to achieve any balance between professionals who work with industry and those who work with unions, even though these consultants consistently take different approaches to the establishment of TLVs. Finally, they concluded that not only did industry play far too dominant a role in the establishment of TLVs, this role was often hidden from public view, since the affiliations of consultants who work largely with industry are never made public. It is true that the affiliations of pro-labour consultants are also not provided—but these consultants are rarely used.[11]

Castleman and Ziem's research into the history of TLVs points out that when they were first published, the ACGIH made it clear that just because an employer did not exceed the TLVs—or as they were first called, Maximum Allowable Concentrations—there was no guarantee that the workers would be safe. Yet a few years later, without changing the limits or publishing the results of new tests the conference claimed the TLVs were safe for "all" workers—a claim that it modified to "nearly all workers" in 1958. The non-thresholds were turned into thresholds, not by science but by an administrative decision made by an organization that did not have a single physician on the panel that set the TLVs.

The point that Castleman and Ziem underscored was that the setting of limits is very much a political, not a scientific exercise. And since it is political, the people who are going to be affected by the decision most directly—the workers who are exposed to dusts and fumes—must be allowed to participate directly in determining the standards. Unfortunately, they have been largely excluded from this process, which has been dominated by those organizations that have the most to gain from weak regulations.

Eric Tucker notes that in Ontario the practise in the 1980s was for the government to set standards that reflected existing exposure levels. For example,

> Ontario selected a vinyl chloride standard of 2 ppm [parts per million] when, according to the Ministry [of Labour], most of the vinyl chloride industry was already achieving exposure levels below one ppm. With respect to silica, the Ministry set a standard of 0.20 mg/m^3 when its prior guideline was 0.10 mg/m^3 and when 75 percent of mining work sites sampled were already achieving silica exposure levels below the guideline. Indeed, with the possible exception of the coke oven emissions standard, the Ministry has never selected an exposure level which it believed would impose significant compliance costs on industry.[12]

What regulations are likely to do is bring firms that have flagrantly ignored workers' health up to an industry standard. However, the process also serves to legitimate existing conditions. Standards are often set that acknowledge that a certain number of cancers per 100,000 workers is inevitable. In other cases, the standard reflects what is affordable. All of this, of course, presumes that employers are being obliged to meet existing standards; a questionable assumption when the laws are rarely being enforced.

But is it true that punishment is ineffective? Perhaps the clearest answer to that question comes from John Braithwaite, who studied coal mining safety enforcement in Britain, the United States and Australia. It is important to point out that Braithwaite rejects the idea that the state must either punish or persuade. The evidence he has examined makes it clear that both punishment and persuasion are part of an effective health and safety strategy. But it is equally clear that punishment can be quite effective in saving lives.

Many employers argue that they are tied up in irrelevant, government-imposed health and safety rules that shackle productivity and protect workers from non-existent hazards. But in the coal mining industry accidents rarely occur without there being a violation of the health and safety laws. Some studies show that in four of every five accidents a health and safety law had been broken. And when one looks only at serious accidents the likelihood of a law being broken is even higher.

Not only do violations cause accidents, it appears that inspections make workplaces safer. Studies show that in Britain and the U.S., accident rates have fallen every time the government has passed legislation that increased the regulation of mines. The only time this did not happen was in 1952, when the U.S. government passed a tough bill, but did not provide the funding needed to improve enforcement. As Braithwaite notes, "the most dramatic periods and places of improvement have been associated with the strengthening of government enforcement efforts."[13]

But how do inspectors make these improvements—by punishment or by persuasion? Braithwaite points out that the periods in which U.S. and British accidents fell most rapidly were those periods in which governments were making the greatest use of punishment as opposed to persuasion. But he warns against basing too firm a conclusion on these statistics. After all, he notes, inspectors who punish are also likely to be persuading as well.

One might ask, aren't progressives being hypocritical when they call for the state to take a more aggressive approach to punishing corporate criminals? After all, are we not the original bleeding hearts, opposing the death penalty and advocating mediation and reconciliation rather than locking street punks up and throwing away the key? Liberals are the ones who say that the death penalty, let alone longer jail sentences, do not serve as an effective deterrent. To be fair, shouldn't the left be supporting a conciliatory, educational approach to violations of health and safety law?

In fact, there is nothing hypocritical in calling for a more aggressive approach to enforcing health and safety laws while supporting restorative justice approaches in other cases. Many of the arguments against taking punitive approaches to crime do not apply in the case of corporate crime. A youthful street criminal is likely to have a criminal self-image, give very little thought to the future, and apply little rationality to a decision to break into a house or mug a defenseless senior citizen. For these reasons, law and order solutions do little to reduce criminal activities. Corporations and the people who direct them are forward looking, do not view themselves as criminals, and attempt to make all decisions on a rational basis. When faced with a state that takes a punitive approach to health and safety violation, a corporation is likely to obey the law. In other words, punishment is likely to do a better job of deterring corporate criminals than street criminals.

Braithwaite does not believe that every health and safety violation ought to be prosecuted. Indeed, there are many situations where he believes that persuasion is a far more appropriate response. Without a mixture of the two strategies inspectors would find themselves bogged down in prosecution, while corporations might find it more expedient to drag cases through the courts rather than comply with the law. As Braithwaite concludes:

> The power to punish helps give legitimacy to regulators who wish to persuade. One is inclined to listen to the persuasive overtone of an inspector if the consequence of not listening is his replacing the velvet glove with the iron fist.[14]

But is that really an iron fist in the velvet glove? Let's go back to the story of Melford Nickoshie, the construction worker who was trapped for hours when a trench collapsed. The government did take Kordite Construction to court. And it won its case, a fairly rare event. But the firm was fined only $400 for failing to supervise work during the time workers were in an excavation and another $100 for failing to properly install shoring. For the owners the fine was not only cheap, it was predictable. The previous year there had been only four Manitoba convictions for violating the excavation laws and the average fine was $575, almost exactly the amount that Kordite ended up paying. This is less than a punishment and more of a rather predictable license fee that the firm is required to pay on a semi-regular basis.

Persuasion has always been given a much higher priority than prosecution. In 1951, for example, Manitoba had only five factory inspectors for the entire province, and four of them did not have cars assigned to them.[15] But with the introduction of the internal responsibility system, the role of the factory inspector became even more complicated. After all, the responsibility was now being shifted from the inspector to the joint health-and-safety committee. Rather than serving as a cop, the inspector, in the opinion of many politicians, was now to be a facilitator. If the IRS was working well, one would need fewer inspectors, make less use of prosecution and levy fewer severe fines. One of the results of the introduction of the IRS has been a de-emphasis and reduction of the role of the inspector. Had the IRS represented a real empowering of workers this might have been acceptable. Instead the rhetoric of IRS has been used to cover an actual retreat from what was already a very weak commitment to enforcement.

This retreat is spelled out countless policy books. In the 1990s the Ontario government's *Operations Manual* for inspectors stated, "The first objective of the Minister is to impress upon the parties that success depends upon each person in the workplace assuming required responsibilities and the proper internal functioning of the joint health-and-safety committee, or similar cooperative mechanism." The document goes on to say that when work orders are ignored, prosecutions should be "considered."[16]

The steady withdrawal from external regulation of the workplace continued following the election of Mike Harris in 1995. In its first term the Harris government:

- Dismantled the Workplace Health and Safety Agency;
- Reduced training requirements for health and safety representatives;
- Cut the budgets of the Occupational Health Clinics;
- Laid off occupational health nurses and physicians;
- Closed the Occupational Health Laboratory and Library;
- Disbanded the Occupational Diseases Panel; and
- Disbanded the joint labour/employer toxic substance standard setting process.

Policies will never be implemented if there is no one to implement them. In the 1990s the number of workplace health and safety inspectors remained woefully inadequate. In 1995 British Columbia had the best ratio of inspectors per workers, employing one inspector for every 11,000 workers. Ontario had one inspector for every 20,000 workers, while Alberta with one inspector for every 32,000 workers had the worst ratio in the country.

Nor will they implemented if the government's philosophy is to not implement. As the health and safety officer for the Ontario Public Service Employees' Union, Bob DeMatteo has had a ringside view of the Harris government's destruction of health and safety enforcement. A former New Yorker, DeMatteo approaches his work with an intensity that is almost palpable. He interrupts our interview to call members who he thinks I should talk to, to dig up articles I should read, and to take a steady stream of phone calls. This is more than a job—it's a mission. His father was a construction worker who succumbed to silicosis. DeMatteo believes the disease was the result of employer negligence and lax enforcement.

> What we have seen develop is a culture of non-enforcement. The culture or the concepts that have now evolved are taking the internal responsibility system one step further. The new concepts are self-reliance and self-compliance. So now what you have is the notion that you make the workplace parties self-reliant. Now no one has ever really done that. Self compliance? That means you get the employers to voluntarily comply with the various safety codes or even going beyond those, going to even higher standards that might be voluntarily adopted by the employers.
>
> Frankly it is a Pollyanna idea—although I hesitate to use the word Pollyanna because it assumes that everyone is innocent in dreaming up this scheme. I don't think they are innocent in dreaming up this scheme. I think that what governments have created is a license to kill workers.

When inspectors are told to have employers voluntarily comply with legislation, they are being told that it is their job to cajole the employer into obeying the law. According the DeMatteo the message sent government inspectors is that:

> The last thing you do is use the authority that is granted to you under any particular statute. That you do not use the force of the law that you have available to you. What you do is attempt to persuade people that this is the right thing to do.

This turns the internal responsibility system into the eternal responsibility system. Inspectors stand on the sidelines while employers can delay any action at the committee level by calling for more research.

When I interviewed DeMatteo he was in the midst of fighting a grievance for an inspector who had been suspended for thirty days because an employer had found his behaviour abusive, and complained about him to the labour minister. A printing company was performing maintenance on a large press without first taking the necessary lock-out procedures that would prevent the machine from starting while being maintained. When the inspector came upon this practice, he could have initiated a prosecution. Instead he wrote an order demanding that the company comply with government safety regulations. On return inspection he found the company was still not in compliance. Again he did not prosecute: he did, however, tell the employer that he was making a mockery of the government's policy of voluntary compliance. According to DeMatteo the inspector was verbally aggressive at this point, but he did not shut down the operation or initiate a prosecution. This led to the inspector's suspension. DeMatteo explains:

> Here is an inspector trying to do his job. Trying to follow the culture of cajoling and persuading and now finds himself on the carpet for using those kinds of tactics. Rather than punish you try to persuade. Any time the inspector is trying to be tough with an employer they are going to be viewed as overzealous and lacking in negotiation skills and so on and so forth

Not that fines are all that high in the long run. In 1997 the Manitoba government increased the fines that could be levied against companies convicted of violating workplace health and safety laws. In some cases the new fines were to be ten times higher than the old ones and the maximum penalty jumped from $30,000 to $300,000. On paper it looked like good news for workers. The biggest surprise was the fact that the business community was so quiet about these changes. Business leaders may well have kept their mouths shut because they knew that the courts almost never give the maximum allowable fines. This becomes apparent when one looks at what the courts had been doing prior to the fines being increased.

In April 1997, the extermination firm N.L. Poulin, Ltd. was convicted of three offenses. For failing to inform the government of an accident it was fined $2,500; for failing to monitor a worker's exposure to a product which left him permanently disabled it was fined $2,500; and for failing to inform workers on the proper use, storage, and handling of the product it was fined $500. (That last figure shows just how much significance the courts place on the need to respect a worker's right to know.) This was just about the largest fine that has ever been levied in Manitoba. The VK Mason Construction firm was fined $10,000 in November 1990 when a worker died in an accident, Oakwood Roofing was fined $3,000 when a worker died, Palliser Furniture was fined $5,000 even though there were no fatalities, and PowerVac was fined $10,000 following a fire that nearly killed a worker. And that is it for big fines in Manitoba in the 1990s. They almost all involve cases where workers are killed or seriously injured. Fines ought to be just as high in cases where workers are not killed or seriously injured as in cases where they are. The fines should be imposed for violating the laws—for putting people's lives at risk. Yet the only time the stick comes down is when the risk turns into reality.

But perhaps there are no violations. It would be unfair to chastise a system for its low level of prosecutions if there were in fact very few perpetrators. In fact, infractions abound. First of all, in 1997 only 47 percent of the firms that were required to have health and safety committees were actually submitting committee minutes to the government, as required. The Manitoba Mines Inspection Branch issued 863 improvement orders in 1997-98 and 1,010 the following year. [17] If the government had chosen to use the iron fist in these cases there would have been far more than the eighteen prosecutions that were undertaken in 1997-98 or the five in 1998-99.

And all of this suggests a very different question: should employers who violate health and safety laws be sent to jail for violating the criminal code?

ONE DAY IN THE 1970s York University law professor Harry Glasbeek was giving his standard lecture on occupational safety and health law. As a former labour lawyer in Canada and Australia, it was a topic he had some familiarity with, although it had never been his specialty. Looking at the figures he had just put on the blackboard outlining the number of accidents and deaths that were directly attributable to work every year, he felt suddenly overwhelmed.

> It made me exclaim in class, "Why don't we prosecute the people who are causing this?" My class, of course, comprised of law students, went ape. They thought this was an outrageous idea. They hoped to graduate and represent the people I wanted to prosecute.

This response only further fueled Glasbeek's enthusiasm. Since then much of his writing and research has focused on the use of the criminal law in health and safety cases. His research culminated in a course he taught called The Corporation As Criminal.

He believes that a campaign to make greater use of criminal law in health and safety cases would expose some of the myths and misconceptions that stand in the way of improving workplace health and safety. Chief among these is the view that health and safety regulation must not be so stringent as to limit a company's profitability. If it could be shown that certain profit-making activities would be considered criminal if they took place outside the workplace, Glasbeek argues that it would be easier to regulate those activities. (Killing children might serve as an example. In the summer of 2000 a 14-year-old boy died in a construction accident in Alberta. The story ran in the *Globe and Mail* on an inside page, meriting only a few paragraphs. After all, he was working legally with his parents' permission. However, a few years ago when a motorcycle gang war bomb blast killed a young boy in Montreal, the story made the front pages for days. In the end government modified the criminal code to make it easier to prosecute gangs. One death was an accident, one a horrible crime: much of the difference comes from the fact that we are prepared to tolerate deaths from a profitable construction industry.)

In this century criminal law has been used less than a dozen times against employers in health and safety-related matters, and few of those cases withstood an employer appeal. Glasbeek says that this is because it is believed that employers and workers have mutually and freely entered into an employment agreement. If something goes wrong, it is unfair to prosecute the employer—after all, the worker was there of his or her own free will. This is different from someone who is robbed or hit by a drunk driver—it is clear that in those cases no consent has been given. The other main argument against the use of criminal law involves the concept of intent (or as it is referred to in legal circles, *mens rea,* or having the guilty act in mind). Before a person can be charged with a criminal act, they must not only have done the deed, they had to have an intent to do the deed. Under Canadian law corporations are not held criminally liable unless it is possible to prove that a senior corporate official ordered the act and did so with a guilty intent. The fact that corporate leaders have created a culture in which lower level managers know that they must sacrifice safety for the sake of production is not sufficient.

Glasbeek takes the position that workers do not freely choose to perform unhealthy work. Their decisions are always shaded by the threat of unemployment.

> We pretend that workers have agreed to the risk in the workplace. Now the risk in the workplace is something like a one in ten chance people will be injured on the job. Now that varies across occupations. In some occupations the incidence of injury is much higher. Lawyers and treasury officials are quite safe in their work, whereas miners and loggers are quite unsafe in their work. But on the average there is a 10 percent chance of getting hurt. Let's take that average seriously. I am sitting in the CBC studios in Toronto. Next door is the Skydome. It holds, I don't know, 50,000 people

1 I18 *Consulted to Death*

when full. Imagine if the Skydome people said, "Come and view our spectacle. You can enter free. And we will give you a hot dog to enjoy.

"But at half time, there is a minor risk. Somebody will come out with a submachine gun and just fire randomly and hurt 5,000 of you. Some will be only nicked, some will be seriously injured and some will die. But if you take that risk, you can keep the hotdog."

It is my suspicion that very few people would show up to see the spectacle given those risks. And that is the risk that we ask workers to take in the workplace—they are supposed to agree to come to a workplace where they have a one in ten chance of getting nicked, seriously hurt or killed, but they can keep their wages. That is the bargain that we pretend we make with them as a voluntary bargain. I don't think the Skydome would be full of people under that arrangement, but people are clamoring to get into our workplaces, which tells you something about the inequality we have in our bargain.

Glasbeek usually asks leave to bore his listener with a few facts. The inequality he is speaking of is deep and has been growing. By the late 1990s the richest 10 percent of the Canadian population controlled 57 percent of the nation's wealth, while 40 percent of the population controlled less than 1 percent of its wealth. Glasbeek points out that it is the richest 10 percent that has the opportunity to determine how work is going to be done, where it is going to be done, and who is to be employed. And they will receive any profits that arise. It is the members of the other 40 percent who agree to do the work. They are also the ones who run all the risk of being injured on the job. Those who control only 1 percent of the nation's wealth have little choice but to agree to the Skydome scenario that Glasbeek has outlined.

What about intention? Glasbeek recognizes that employers want to make profits, not kill workers. Yet there are many examples in which the criminal law is used to successfully prosecute people who never intended to hurt anyone. People who voluntarily embark on dangerous courses of conduct leading to the injury of another person have been found guilty of criminal negligence. Warming to his argument Glasbeek says,

> If I get into my car after drinking a great deal and I then wipe out some unsuspecting person on the road, I will be held criminally responsible. That is not even a question. Everybody agrees with that. And the reason for that is not because I intended to hurt somebody, it is because I drank knowing I was going to drive. That is, I didn't care whether I hurt anybody. That is why I am being held criminally responsible.

It may be argued that in some cases the employer is not doing anything to hurt workers, but that the lack of action is itself what is doing harm—for example, if the air is polluted because the company has not installed a proper ventilation system. However, there are a variety of laws that require workplaces to be maintained in a safe and healthy fashion. Beyond this, Glasbeek points out that it only takes a slight bit of rewriting to turn any failure to take action into an action. For example, if the employer has failed to put in proper ventilation, he is putting too much dust into the atmosphere. One of the charges that Glasbeek recommends staying away from is murder, which he thinks would be difficult to prove and could lead to a misuse of the law in other areas.[18]

But which laws would be used? In a paper that he wrote with Susan Rowland, Glasbeek set out to answer the question whether it is a crime for employers to kill and injure workers on the job. His answer was a resounding yes. Among the available criminal charges that could, he believes, be plausibly brought against various employers are criminal negligence, assault causing bodily harm, mischief, the rather archaic-sounding law against the laying of traps, and conspiracy.

Glasbeek is well aware that his students would not be the only ones to go ape if the criminal law were used this way. But he welcomes opposition, since most of it underscores his political point, namely that "behaviour becomes less heinous when it is part of conduct engaged in with a so-called enterprise motive." In health and safety matters companies are allowed to argue that they cannot meet standards without losing their competitive advantage. But criminals are not allowed to argue that they would go broke if they didn't rob banks. Other arguments are likely to be raised—for example, if employers were regularly the subject of criminal investigations they would likely treat inspectors in a much more hostile fashion. They would go to much greater lengths to keep information from them and to refuse to cooperate unless forced to do so. This may be so, but this is what all criminals do—and the state does not forego prosecuting them because it is difficult.

But who should be fined or sent to jail when a corporation is prosecuted? The shareholders received the profits, but they know nothing about the company's day-to-day operations. They are simply passive investors. Glasbeek turns this argument on its head. He points out that if an outside investor were to attempt to harm the corporation by means of a hostile takeover, investors would take action to either support or fend off the bid. Lawyers, accountants, and financial advisers would hunt them down and provide them with the briefing they would need to determine the corporation's future. That being the case, the state ought to hunt them down and hold them responsible if their corporation is killing and maiming workers.

Aside from his recommendation against charging employers with murder, Glasbeek is prepared to put another limitation on the use of the criminal law. He points out that there are in fact certain occasions when it is permissible to inflict pain and injury on another person. Boxing and wrestling, for example, are legal. However, there are special licenses for these events and there are even limits as to what can be done in the ring. Current health and safety laws should be viewed as the bare minimum that is required of employers. In other words, when they come to work employees are agreeing to accept no risks above and beyond the legislated limits. Glasbeek stops for a second to observe that in reality,

> That's a lie since the employment contract is not really a voluntary contract. But let's pretend it is. Then the employer should be allowed to hurt workers if he stays within the government rules. Above those rules we should lay criminal charges because the contract is now no longer valid, it is against public policy.

A private member's bill that would make it easier to prosecute corporations was introduced in 1999 by New Democratic Party leader Alexa McDonough. The bill would also make the directors of such corporations criminally liable and create a new corporate crime: "failing to provide safe working conditions." While such bills rarely have success, the United Steelworkers has, with the support of NDP labour critic Pat Martin, engaged in a very successful lobbying campaign in favour of this bill.

Glasbeek has become a favourite at health and safety conferences. Following the Westray disaster and the failed prosecution of the Westray management, Glasbeek's moral fervour and gift for analogy guaranteed his message a warm welcome. However, not all activists believe that the solution lies in more prosecutions. A brief prepared by Ontario inspectors pointed out that court actions are time-consuming, expensive and non-productive. Often the Crown would take a case to court without first interviewing the inspector involved in the case, agreeing to a plea bargain that the inspector believed to be insufficient. The inspectors pointed to alternative approaches in the United States and Sweden—two countries not normally seen as having anything in common when it comes to social policy. Both countries allow inspectors to assess fines without resort to the courts. And while employers can appeal the fines, the bodies that hear the appeals are not always judicial and their rulings are final.

Colin Lambert, the Canadian Union of Public Employee's long-time health and safety director, has positive things to say about the American approach where inspectors have the power to assess fines on the spot.

> What they do is they assess how long those violations have been going on and how many workers were involved. And for every day they assess them the minimum. Often that runs up to seven or eight million dollars. That is quite a severe stick to be threatened with, seven or eight million dollars, even for a huge company. And what they then tell the companies, particularly the ones that have sites right across the United States, is "We expect you to have policies and programs in place that will stop these violations. And we expect them right across your company. And if not we starting counting again from today."

The British Columbia government takes a similar approach. There the Workers' Compensation Board has the authority to levy additional assessments on companies that violate health and safety laws. Since these are not fines, but compensation assessments, they are not dealt with through the court system. Unlike in a criminal case, the inspectors do not only have to prove their case beyond a shadow of a doubt. The increased assessments deal with the risk created, rather than the damage caused. This distinction is significant, since judges often hand down low fines—in instances where health and safety laws were violated yet no one was injured. Unlike in criminal cases, it is permissible to bring the company's previous health and safety record into consideration.

Even Bob Sass expresses ambivalent feelings about enforcement. At the outset, he says, he was zealous in his approach to enforcement. "In the early period, from 1972 to 1976, I probably had the best record in Canada regarding enforcement of health and safety. I had a policy of prosecuting whenever there was a fatality." But over time he came to lose his faith in the effectiveness of prosecution.

> It took a lot of effort and time. What would happen, even after a fatality, is that you would move to enforce, you would prosecute, and then there may be a fine of $2,500. Sometimes less, and you have to tell the widow or the family that this was the outcome of the death of a loved one. It was an insult; it just became part of their grief.

After Sass left the government he worked with Connie and Miles Greenwood, whose nineteen-year-old son, Jason Greenwood, was killed while putting up power lines for the Saskatchewan Telephone Service. The family mounted a lengthy public campaign that eventually led to the prosecution and conviction of the company for fifty-two health and safety violations. The corporation was fined $7,000. "This devastated Connie Greenwood and Miles, her husband. Now what are we talking about here? We are talking about two or three years of organizing, mobilizing, establishing a defence fund, which was over twenty thousand dollars with contributions from activists and health and safety people in the province." According to Sass, the trial judge recommended that criminal charges be pressed against the company but despite the family's efforts the case was stayed.

The arguments against reliance upon the criminal law are not without merit. That there has been only a handful of successful prosecutions of an employer on charges of criminal negligence, manslaughter or murder relating to the death of workers in Canadian history.[19] It might be argued that more could be achieved by giving inspectors the right to levy fines on the job rather than by opening up a process that would take years and render unsatisfactory results. But the same argument could be made about any aspect of the criminal law. It is a slow process, it requires tremendous resources, and its results can be uneven. However, unless we truly believe that law-breaking is less criminal when it is a by-product of profit-making, we ought to insist that it be subjected to criminal sanction and that the state commit the appropriate level of resources to ensure that prosecutions are conducted in a timely and thorough manner.

6

THE SYSTEM MUST BE FIRST

THE THRUST OF THIS BOOK'S ARGUMENT is that the changes of twenty-five years ago did not go far enough. They did not address the underlying power imbalances at work. The three rights are weak rights. The right to participate in misnamed—in the end it is the right to be consulted. This is not necessarily a criticism of the people who introduced those rights or the workers who embraced them. These rights were improvements, won only after historic struggle. Furthermore, there are thousands of workplace health and safety activists across the country who make use of these rights every day. They are not fools and they are not misguided. Nor are they without accomplishment. The committee process is, as Gerry Adolphe noted, quite effective in addressing many ongoing issues, particularly if they do not directly affect production costs. The new system has improved communication, and this has allowed for more effective handling of many hazards. But it has not lived up to its promise to make work more democratic, or to provide workers with more control over their jobs.

There are many, particularly in management, who would say, So what? Work is not meant to be democratic, just safe and healthy. Workers who are asking for control are simply asking for too much. Despite all the talk of employee empowerment, employers have kept a firm hold on their right to determine what gets made and how it gets made. This sort of power is doled out to employees in dribs and drabs. But it turns out that decision-making is not a frill; it is intrinsic to the issue of workplace health and safety. We can see this when we look at how modern technological innovations affect workplace health.

IT WAS JUST ANOTHER TELEPHONE call. As a long-distance operator with the Manitoba Telephone System (MTS), Diane Ives was used to putting through seven hundred such calls every shift. By 1986 she had been doing this work for over a decade. But on this one October night she realized she was having trouble keying the numbers in correctly. "My arm felt as is someone was pressing down on it. And then I realized I must be having some sort of sensation."

Some sort of sensation: that was about as specific as the claims ever got. But in 1986 over eighty MTS workers reported similar experiences. Their symptoms ranged from numbness in their arms, dizziness and disorientation, to static shocks in their headsets. Twice the provincial workplace health and safety department closed down the operation. At one point nearly fifty operators were refusing to work. Frustrated MTS officials went so far as to move all the long-distance terminals out of Winnipeg, but the problems followed them— Diane Ives was working in Selkirk when she experienced her "sensations."

Ives has vivid memories of the evening before the government shut down the operation: "There were six shocks throughout the building. After a while that evening, I have to confess, I was quite afraid. It seemed to me that within an hour we were all going to be fried. It gets away from you and I think were all in a bit of panic. The next day when we went to work and it had been shut down, there was a great deal of relief."

Joanne Swayze never experienced any on-the-job sensations, but she was present when other workers did.

> I was working in the cord board office, and I was just sitting there, when all of a sudden I noticed this person went flying behind me. I turned and looked and she did, she went at least three feet back, and the chair fell over and then I thought, "There is something really strange happening." I worked, but I did not feel comfortable at all. I could not wait to get out of there. But I was sitting there,

tense, waiting, is it going to happen to me? I never got a shock. But
I was certainly ready for one.

The first signs of trouble came early in the morning of January 9,
1986, following a power surge in the MTS building on Winnipeg's
Corydon Avenue. Three directory-assistance operators complained
of humming and tingling sensations in their headsets, and one was
taken to the emergency ward of a local hospital. No health problems
were detected and she was sent home for rest. Within three weeks,
fifty-one more operators reported similar sensations—for lack of a
better term the operators and the telephone company called them
shocks. It was a poor choice of words, leaving the impression that
operators were being blasted out of their chairs by 120-volt charges.

That mistake was compounded by MTS's decision to have
Winnipeg neurologist Michael Newman examine some of the
operators. Finding no sign of electrical shock, Newman concluded
that "the whole thing is an elaborate hoax." Newman went public
with his conclusions, outraging the operators. Union representative
Howie Raper said that MTS managers were also reporting similar
sensations when they worked the machines. "If it is a hoax, it is a
conspiracy of managers, workers and the union," he said, making it
clear he doubted that such a conspiracy could ever come to fruition.

Angry operators felt they were being portrayed as a bunch of
hypocritical hypochondriacs. Although none of the electrical engineers brought in by MTS could find serious electrical faults, the
operators rejected any suggestion that the problem could in any way
be stress-related. Which wasn't surprising. As one operator noted, "stress
is never the issue, it is always your ability to deal with stress."

Full service was restored by late February 1986, but operators
continued to register minor complaints throughout the spring. After
months of study, a five-member medical panel—with a number of
union appointees—could only conclude that the probable source
was a "buildup and slow discharge of electro-static energy," with little
significant health risk. But the issue did not go away.

In late September the incidents spread from the directory-assistance unit to the long-distance operators, prompting an immediate

walkout. Operator Carol Klagenburg recalled that night vividly.

> The directory assistance office got the shocks, the toll office had heard about it. I think somebody had a customer who had to call director assistance and said to the long distance operator, "Hey, guess what, somebody got a shock." The long distance operators, and there had to be at least a dozen of us—unplugged and said to management, "We don't want this to happen to us, we are not going to work unless it is safe."

While the operators were exercising their right to refuse, Klagenburg said that even if the right had not existed they would have refused to work. However, the right provided the operators with a shield if the employer tried to accuse them of staging an illegal wildcat strike. By October 3, forty operators were refusing to work, and one operator had fainted on the job. MTS moved its long-distance stations out of the city and brought in another army of engineers and experts. But still no technical problems could be identified.

Very gingerly some union advisers began to raise the possibility the problems were stress related. Dr. Annalee Yassi, a physician with the Manitoba Federation of Labour's Occupational Health Centre, had long wondered if the problem did not relate to the way work was organized at MTS. Whenever she raised this issue, however, she was very careful to make it clear she was not repeating Newman's accusations. In an interview at the time she said, "This has nothing to do with emotional instability. The pain and discomfort people are feeling are very real and very distressing. People are not making this up, it is not imaginary, it is not a hoax."

Yassi was right to be apprehensive. Joanne Swayze recalls that she was not happy when Yassi first suggested the problem might be work organization.

> It was a Friday afternoon. I had just come back to see an ambulance driving away from the building and an operator had been taken out. Workplace health and safety was there and in a very short period of time the office had been shut down. I am not sure when Dr. Yassi arrived on the premises, but she met with the union

rep. and myself, and took us away to a quiet little corner and said, "Look, this is stress." I just absolutely rejected that. I felt betrayed by Dr. Yassi. She was with the MFL Occupational Health Centre, she was supposed to be on my side. And here she is coming up with somewhat the same scenario as Dr. Newman was hinting at. I didn't believe it. ... [But] she was right—she hit the nail on the head early on.

When people did begin to look at work organization what they saw was not pretty. The work was regimented, regulated, and continuous. Any operator who wanted to go to the bathroom had to phone a supervisor and ask permission. The worker would be put on a list and phoned back when her turn had come up. A computer scanned each operator's position every ten seconds to see if they were on the job. Computers were used for everything—including scheduling. Because the computers could predict when the periods of high usage would be, shifts were fragmented and broken up to fit around call patterns. It was not uncommon for a worker to have a different shift for each day of the week, and a different set of shifts the following week, playing havoc with operators' family lives. Many operators said they were treated as being less than human. "We could not talk to one another. There are little partitions between us and we would jack our chairs up high to talk over the partitions to one another."

Telecommunications had undergone a tremendous technical revolution in the 1980s. And none of those changes were being used to improve the operators' working conditions. Where they once used to handle each call from beginning to end, now they would handle only a portion of each call. They did not answer the phone, instead incoming calls were automatically fed into their headsets one after another. Finely tuned staffing levels ensured that there would never be so many operators on duty that an operator could count on a few quiet moments.

The operators were expected to deal with calls in an average of twenty seconds—and computers were able to calculate whether or not they were meeting this standard. As one operator said, "So there was always an invisible whip, you have to speed up, you have to work faster." But the computer did not replace more old-fashioned methods of supervision. Operators were also listened to remotely—what one operator called "the famous eavesdropping. What management was looking for there was mistakes. They were not looking for what you were doing right, they were looking for what you were doing wrong. It was not unusual to have that supervisor come up to you and say, 'Ah ha. I caught you.'"

One of the operators' major complaints focused on ways in which rules limited the quality of the service they could provide to customers. These rules were based on the assumption that each worker was only supposed to perform a limited function or only provide certain information. For example, only long distance operators could give out area codes. Joanne Swayze explained that if a local information operator was asked for the Toronto area code, she was not supposed to provide the information—even if she knew it. Instead her job was to "get that customer to call long-distance to get that information, the reason being not all directory assistance operators might know that and therefore this customer would call back and expect the same service." And if they gave the number, they might end up in trouble. Carol Klagenburg recalled:

> A service assistant would be monitoring my calls. And she said I am going to have to charge you with four failures. I said what did I do wrong. She said, you quoted this area code and before you do that you have to say, "To my personal knowledge this is the area code."

Even the supervisors had very little power to change the way work was structured. Changes in scheduling, for example, were beyond their control. The work was automated, repetitive, routine, and closely measured.

The tensions and conflicts that arose when workers began reporting shocks compounded these problems. Many workers said they did not report sensations because they did not want to be seen as crazy or malingerers. While many managers sympathized with the operators, they were also under pressure to bring the issue to a close, and were always operating under the suspicion that it was some sort of hoax.

The review team Yassi worked with eventually concluded that the main problem was a "collective stress reaction." Management and the union at MTS introduced a variety of changes, all aimed at providing operators with more control over their working lives. These changes did result in the end of the reported incidents. Looking back on the event, Yassi said that one of the problems was the medical community's unwillingness to use stress as anything other than an explanation of last resort—only to be used when no other physical cause can be detected. "Physicians should recognize that the psychosocial effects of technology may be more devastating than the potential physical hazards with which technology is sometimes associated." Newman's dismissal of the events as a hoax increased worker resistance to any explanation that was not physical since they believed "a physical cause was necessary for their vindication."[1]

When I interviewed a group of telephone operators in the summer of 1994 it appeared that the story had a happy ending. Workers had been given more input into scheduling, their knowledge was being given greater respect, and the eavesdropping had been done away with. But there is no halting progress. In 1997 the provincial Conservative government privatized MTS. Since then management has been aggressively downsizing: the workplace reforms are things of the past, as operators are once more driven by technology. On-the-job stress is now coupled with the very real fear that most of the operator jobs will simply be shipped out of the province.

THE IMPACT OF WORK organization on Manitoba telephone operators is just one example of how deeply the links between work and health run. The problems did not arise from a lack of protective devices or exposure to dangerous substances. All the laws were being obeyed, no threshold limits were being ignored. The technology was cutting edge and information-based. The MTS experience should not be seen as a freak occurrence, however. Rather, it is an example of how illness is designed into our jobs.

Over the past two decades the New England-based researcher

Robert Karasek and the Danish physician Töres Theorell have been studying the link between what they call psychosocial health and job organization. Much of their work focuses on the long-term health impacts—particularly increases in heart disease—of work-related stress. Karasek and Theorell note that for many years researchers ignored workplace stress as a research topic. That was because it was thought stress would be particularly prevalent among managers and that this executive stress would lead to higher rates of heart disease among people with more social status. But researchers concluded that executives did not have abnormal rates of heart disease—and that ended most research into heart disease and work.

Karasek and Theorell turned the prevailing wisdom on its head. They concluded that it is the bossed, not the bosses, who suffer from workplace stress. The key to their research was an examination of how much control a worker has over his or her job. In their research, jobs are classified on the basis of the demands that are being placed upon the worker and the worker's ability to determine how she or he will respond to those demands. They ended up with four different job types. In the active job, the demands on the worker are quite high but the worker has considerable leeway in determining how to meet the challenge. Surgeons and professional athletes fall into this category. In low-strain jobs workers do not have to meet high demands and they have considerable control over how they do meet those demands. Repair personnel fit into this category. Workers in both these categories tend to enjoy better mental and physical health than the rest of the workforce.

Jobs with a low-level of demand and little decision-making latitude are called passive jobs. These include such work at being a watchman or janitor. These workers may experience a loss of skills and have little interest in their work, but they do not have significantly elevated rates of heart disease. Finally, there are the high-strain jobs. These are jobs in which the workers experience constant demands, but do not have many or any options about how they are to respond to these demands. There is but one way to the job and they must do it that way. Assembly-line workers leap to mind, and so do telephone operators. Karasek and Theorell found that workers who fall into this category are far more likely to suffer from heart disease than workers in the other three types of jobs.

They noted that workers in high-stress jobs lack the freedom to employ many of the normal strategies that people use—unconsciously—to relieve stress. They cannot talk to one another, they can only relax at prescribed times. Often they cannot even fidget. These are all wasteful activities that have been eliminated from contemporary jobs. Some stress is unavoidable—family members will become sick, natural disasters will take place. And some of the stress in some jobs will always be there—health-care professionals must deal with the ill and the dying, social workers must work with people in trouble. But it turns out that, as long as workers have some ability to control the way they respond to these stresses, they are not that unhealthy. Karasek and Theorell write,

> The primary work-related risk factor appears to be lack of control over how one meets the job's demands and how one uses one's skills. In many cases, elevation of risk with a demanding job appears only when these demands occur in interaction with low control on the job. Other research has shown that regular physical exertion has positive effects on cardiovascular health in many situations (although physical hazards can of course pose major health threats beyond our stress perspective). Thus, in our research findings it is not the demands of work itself but the organizational structure of work that plays the most consistent role in the development of stress-related illness.[2]

The good news then is that only one of the four different types of jobs lead to higher levels of heart disease. The bad news is that this one type of job, the high-demand, low-control job, has been the model for most forms of work in industrial societies for the past century. Once these sorts of jobs were found mainly in manufacturing, the prototype being Henry Ford's assembly line worker. However, by the late twentieth century computerization made it possible to spread this highly routinized form of work to every sector of the economy. Karasek and Theorell are right when they say that stress has been designed into work. To see just how right they are it is necessary to poke around in the history of what was once known as scientific management.

IN 1879 THE 23-YEAR-OLD Frederick Winslow Taylor was promoted to the position of gang boss in the Midvale Steel Company in Philadelphia. It was perhaps one of the most significant promotions in the history of management. Taylor had been raised in a wealthy and genteel family. After graduating from a private academy he had passed the Harvard University entrance examinations. But instead of going to Harvard he went to work at Midvale, first as an apprentice pattern maker and then as a machinist. He got the job through family connections, and the apprenticeship was meant to serve as the first step to a career as an engineer—and indeed Taylor did become an engineer. He would seek to re-engineer the way work was done and in so doing became the first management guru.

Throughout his apprenticeship Taylor became aware of the fact that skilled workers were capable of producing more than they did. They did this even if they were paid on a piecework basis, which on the face of it should have encouraged them to work as fast as possible. They restricted output for a number of reasons. First of all, if the work was all done too quickly they might be laid off. Second, they had learned through bitter experience that as they increased production (and their take-home pay) employers would simply cut the pay rate. When this happened they wound up earning the same amount and working faster. Finally, skilled craft workers worked at what they believed to be a respectable pace. They were not interested in wearing themselves out on the job. Each workshop had its own pace of work—and a new worker who tried to work faster was despised as a rate-buster. His tools often went missing and his work was mysteriously spoiled. Eventually the discipline of the shop brought him under control. As an apprentice, young Fred Taylor was intimately aware of the ways in which workers restricted production. The name for this practice was soldiering, coming from the sailor's pejorative for soldiers at sea, who were treated as passengers.

Taylor was deeply offended by soldiering. On becoming gang boss he announced to the workers that despite the fact that he had been their friend, he intended to increase production to the levels that he believed they were capable of meeting. First he tried to cajole them into working faster. When that failed, he decided to bully them into it. The men who could not meet his production standards were fired. Taylor stood firm on this, and many men passed through the Midvale machine shop as a result. To his chagrin, he found that he could not grind the sort of improvements that he was looking for out of the men. It was the darkest moment of his young life. Years later he said:

> I was a young man in years, but I give you my word I was a great deal older than I am now, what with the worry, meanness, and contemptibleness of the whole damn thing. It's a horrid life for any man to live, not being able to look any workman in the face without seeing hostility.[3]

From this point on Taylor devoted his life to a search for new techniques of management that would allow him to achieve the revolution that he knew was possible and to bring an end to the hatred between employer and employee. His methods allowed for tremendous increases in production, and guaranteed that the hostility between employer and employee would continue unabated. The problem was implicit in Taylor's motto, "In the past the man has been first. In the future the System must be first."

Taylor's apprenticeship had given him an insight into the skilled craft workers' knowledge and skills. In the late nineteenth century, most factories were little more than large workshops in which skilled workers completed specific projects for the employer, who provided them with raw materials and usually, but not always, the tools of the trade. The manager had only the slightest idea how each job was done or how long it would take to do it. The skilled worker's power lay in his knowledge. As the American radical trade unionist Big Bill Haywood delighted in saying, the boss's brains were under the worker's cap. Taylor intended to perform a nothing less than lobotomy coupled with a brain transplant.

He did not invent time-and-motion study, but he used it

incessantly. He and his assistants spent years timing workers with the dreaded stop-watches that were just coming on the market. At first they timed whole jobs, but they soon came to break each job down into individual components and timed these. These elements would be the building block for each job. From them they could reconstruct the job to find the fastest way to perform the task at hand. For Taylor it was all part of the "gathering in of all the great mass of traditional knowledge which in the past has been in the heads of the workmen."[4]

Once he had determined the best way to do the job, it was outlined in a series of task cards. If the observations had been done correctly, the boss—or the army of white-collar workers that was hired to implement this new scientific management, as Taylor called it—now had access to the worker's brains. And if they played their cards right, future generations of workers would be cut off from that knowledge since it would no longer be passed down through the apprentice system. Instead workers would simply perform their limited tasks. As Taylor, who would have lasted five minutes in a Taylorized workplace, told one employer who sought his advice, his system rested on two principles:

1st. Absolutely rigid and inflexible standards throughout your establishment.

2nd. That each employee of your establishment should receive every day clear-cut, definite instructions as to just what he is to do and how he is to do it, and these instructions should be exactly carried out, whether they are right or wrong.[5]

The last thing Taylor wanted was workers exercising their own judgement. "In our scheme, we do not ask for the initiative of our men. We do not want any initiative. All we want of them is to obey the orders we give them, do what we say, and do it quick."[6]

Like modern-day management gurus, Taylor developed a series of anecdotes that he used again and again in his speeches and writings. The most famous concerns the labourer Henry Noll, who Taylor always identified in his stories as Schmidt. When Taylor was working for the Bethlehem steel company he became involved in a plan to dramatically increase the productivity of the labourers who were loading pig iron into rail cars. Traditionally, the men had loaded about 12.5 tons a day each. Taylor got a team of ten workers together and told them to load a car as fast as they could. Based on their perform-ance he concluded that men could load 71 tons a day. He then reduced that figure to 45 tons (although Taylor was never able to give a reason for this reduction other than an appeal to his own judge-ment or reason—a rather unscientific explanation).

He then asked for ten volunteers. They were told that if they could load 45 tons a day they would be paid $1.69 an hour, rather than the $1.15 they currently received. After the ten realized what they had got themselves into they refused—and were fired. Five more volunteers were found. Two quit after the first day. Two others quit shortly thereafter. The only one left standing was Henry Noll. Noll had to work exactly to the formula that was laid down by Taylor. He received a 60 percent pay increase, but he was moving 360 percent more pig iron. By maintaining this fierce pace, the company was able to reduce the number of yard labourers from six hundred to 140. It should be noted that Taylor's telling of this story changed over time—and with each telling Taylor increased the extent of Noll's accom-plishments.[7]

Labour historian Bryan Palmer notes that Noll paid exactly the sort of price that Karasek and Theorell would predict. Noll was in some senses a very well adjusted worker pre-Taylor. He went into his workplace regularly, he did his job, he produced adequately, the company made a profit off of his work. When it was over he went home and tended to his garden. He was actually building himself and his family their own home. He was a devoted family man.

> Once he had adapted to Taylor's regime his wages were greater. But his quality of life seemed to decline quite dramatically. He gave up on his garden. He gave up on building his house. He spent most of his leisure and undoubtedly a great deal of that extra wage sitting in a pub. In essence it seems that someone who had a rounded life, and worked for a wage and produced adequately, had been

turned into a productive machine, paid slightly better, but who quickly lost the zest for much of living outside the workplace.

In his own career Taylor enjoyed mixed results. He developed a steel that could cut at very high speeds, designed his own golf clubs (his two-handed putter was eventually banned), and invested successfully in a number of enterprises. However, the pulp and paper mill that he managed did not make money, and the Bethlehem Steel Company eventually fired him because his reforms never lived up to their billing. Taylor always believed that his setbacks arose from employers' unwillingness to completely adopt his systems of management. But despite these failures his system caught on. Luck, circumstance and a dose of good public relations made him a successful management consultant. Just as all of today's corporations believe in continuous improvement and the quality of working life, the corporations of a century ago all began experimenting with one or another aspect of scientific management. And even if it was impossible to break every job down to its component parts, elimi-nate the unnecessary parts, train an unskilled worker to do only the necessary parts, and then supervise the worker continuously, employers incorporated these approaches into their belief system. The ideal worker was someone who did what he or she was told, was hired to do a specific task and was not valued for additional knowledge. As Taylor oft times told the men he was studying, "You are not being paid to think." In a thousand different ways knowledge was moved from the shop floor to the planning office, and supervision became stricter and focused more on what workers did than on what they produced. As Taylor's most recent biographer Robert Kanigel writes,

> Today it is only modest overstatement to say that we are all Taylorized, that from assembly-line tasks timed to a fraction of a second, to lawyers recording their time by fractions of an hour, to standardized McDonald's hamburgers, to information operators constrained to grant only so many seconds per call, modern life has become Taylorized.[8]

And if Karasek and Theorell are right, then modern work has

been made very unhealthy as well. As they note, Taylor might just as well have been describing their definition of a high-stress job when he outlined the basics of scientific management.

> Consider the profile that has been found to characterize the job at high risk for psychological stress: the job is low in task decision freedom, low in skill level, but high in psychological demands; it is also, as we will see, low in physical exertion and socially isolated from workmates. This stressful job fits, embarrassingly closely, the specific job design goals of Taylor's scientific management. Thus, psychological stress may easily be the direct, if unintended, outcome of application of these job design philosophies.[9]

Taylor's critics suspected this from the outset. They feared that workers would become automatons once the boss had scooped out their brains. John Mitchell, the president of the United Mine Workers, opposed Taylorism because he thought it would drive workers crazy. He said that the head of the Manhattan State Hospital for the Insane felt that the monotony of work under scientific management was a cause of insanity since the brain cells "finally go dead from lack of use, and then the worker is ready for the insane asylum." Mitchell argued that, "There is nothing so restful as variety."[10] A group of textile workers in 1911 told their union that, "We are pushed to the limit. The mental strain under which we work, and our anxiety and fear that we shall fall below the standard, makes the job scarcely worth while."[11]

But what is it about these high-stress jobs that creates health problems? We don't know all the answers. And it should be noted that heart disease is only one of the major health problems that accompany this sort of work organization. But it is believed that it contributes to long-term factors such as hypertension and arteriosclerosis, and may trigger other forms of coronary heart disease. Stressful work may also aggravate other existing risk factors.[12] Finally, human beings are simply not built to be worked this way. We are essentially social—the "one best way" may also be the least human way of structuring eight hours of our day.

Some people may argue that for the last two decades corporations have been struggling to undo the worst excesses of Taylorism by experimenting with quality of working life and new forms of work organization. These reforms have tended to come to grief as they approach the thorny question of workplace power. Small changes whet everyone's appetites for bigger change, but usually at a certain point, the people on the top panic. That is what happened in Saskatchewan in the early 1980s.

BY THE LATE 1970s BOB SASS was having doubts about the health and safety regime he had helped bring into being. Some of this anxiety stemmed from the model's apparent successes. The manager of the Prince Albert Pulp Company, for example, praised the program. At first, he said, management feared the right to participate would infringe on the employer's "right to manage" and that the whole process would contribute to what he referred to as "creeping unionism." However, the company found the committees were useful tools in reducing accidents and cutting down on absenteeism.[13] By and large in Saskatchewan the workplaces that were supposed to have committees had formed them and they were meeting on a regular basis. As the years progressed, the committees were dealing with more and more problems, although safety issues tended to outnumber health concerns by a two-to-one ratio. Furthermore, one study in the early 1980s suggested that the committees were dealing with 90 percent of the issues that were coming forward. Obviously Sass had no problems with the idea of cutting down on accidents, but his had been a broader vision. He had hoped the committees would be able to chip away at the bedrock of management rights and look at broad issues such as the pace of work, skill levels, and workplace monotony. But little progress had been made in rebalancing power relations in the workplace.

Knowledge remained contested terrain. Experts, and those who could afford to hire experts, were still in control of the system. The knowledge that workers had from their own experience was discounted in the face of technical research papers. Those with access to technical resources were able to manipulate the direction that the committee took. When there was uncertainty, management could always call for more study. This, as Sass saw it, put workers in the world of the meantime.

> What do you do in the meantime. Well you get your studies. And then you have to get them interpreted. And then they get their studies, and then there are differences. Then we try and find out if these studies were done by researchers with company sponsorships leading to predictable results. And then we say, "Well we have to then have our own study. Because in this particular workplace it is unique or the paint is not the same because there is a new element." So now we have to wait for a period of time until the protein tissue study or the effects on rhesus monkeys or whatever is borne out. What do we do in the meantime? Or if the company changes one of the ingredients in the solvent and it is no longer the same, what do we do in the meantime? Well the meantime is why we have the pain and suffering, the enormous pain and suffering among workers in Canada and elsewhere.

The right to refuse and the right to participate were supposed to address what went on in the meantime. But they did not.

> You can say you cannot act without all the information. The information is already known—when you are dizzy, when you are sick, when you are nauseous. When you see fellow workers over a longer period of time suffering from this, that and the other thing. It is already known. The knowledge is already there in the body and the experience. To lop it off for outside external empirical studies, which are clearly limited, puts workers always in the meantime, or having to endure someplace in their own latency period.

When the meantime finally came to an end there may well be a report that concluded existing work practises needed to change. Sass said there was one argument that management could fall back on to fend off change. This was simply by saying that the solution to the problem was too expensive. He refers to this as economic blackmail, the threat to close a plant down rather than address a health and safety issue. And it can be an effective threat. "Unemployment, to a worker, is an injury just as surely as if she lost her hand in a punch press."

Because of these contradictions between what had been intended and what had resulted, Sass began looking for a way to let workers act in the meantime. The search led him to propose the creation of what he called a Work Environment Board. It would differ from joint health-and-safety committees in a number of ways. It could deal with both accidents and the quality of work. Unlike joint health-and-safety committees, it would have a budget that it could use to commission its own research. And it would have real authority—the decisions it made had to be implemented. These were significant changes. But there was one more to come. The power on the WEB would rest with the workers. Under Sass's proposal, the committee would have an equal number of worker and management representatives, plus a chairperson who would have to be approved by the labour appointees.

With the support of the Steelworkers union and the Energy and Chemical Workers, Sass was able to get the Blakeney government to agree to the establishment of a Work Environment Board at the Potash Corporation of Saskatchewan. Sass himself was elected by the unions to serve as the board's chairperson. The board had the authority to deal with all work environment matters—this extended its authority beyond the reach of traditional health and safety committees, leaving it free to look at the pace of work, work organization, and job design. According to Sass it had the power to address "the power relations in production. Who could tell whom to move, how fast, when and where." The WEB negotiated a fund of $250,000 with the PCS and commissioned $80,000 worth of research.

If the WEB led to improved health and safety in the mines, it would take a simple legislative amendment to transform all joint health-and-safety committees into work environment boards with a labour majority and a research budget funded by the Workers' Compensation Board. According to Sass, "It seemed to me that would be the next stage—to deal with some of the problems that were being identified by occupational health and safety activists in the labour movement across the Canada." But it was not to be.

It soon became clear that Sass and the President of the Potash Corporation had very different ideas of what the WEB should be doing. "Now I think what the president of the mining division had in mind with the work environment board was quality of work life. A kind of participation that gives you a sense of belonging, but there is no transformation of meaningful power." Management had no problem with those proposals that sought to make work more humane, but it resisted initiatives that included participation in the purchase of new technology and in the shaping of technological change. In December 1981 Sass sent a letter to the president of PCS stating that:

> There are those on the Work Environment Board who believe that PCS as a crown corporation represents a regime different from that of private capital. If so, then it ought to have policies different from those of the private potash corporations regarding its workers. One important distinction, we believe, is affording PCS workers a measure of involvement in issues which matter to them. If this is not possible or encouraged, what then is the difference between working for PCS and working for privately owned businesses?[14]

The WEB members found themselves fighting with management over a plan to reward departments with accident-free records since such schemes lead to an underreporting of accidents, rather than a decline in accidents. York University professor Gerry Hunnius was called in to attempt to mediate the conflict between the Board and the Potash Corporation. He eventually wrote a report that supported Sass's vision of what the board should be doing. But the corporation continued to stall.

In April of 1982 the Blakeney government was decimated in a provincial election it had expected to win by a wide margin. Led by Grant Devine, the Conservatives were determined to turn the economy over to the market and let everyone in Canada know that Saskatchewan was open for business. To underline the point, Bob Sass was the first person the Conservatives fired. When PCS management demanded that a new chair be appointed, the labour members refused to replace Sass. PCS then pulled out of the board and the

Devine government made no efforts to resuscitate the experiment.

After the election one of the Conservative critics told Sass, "You know we got rid of the board because we understood what you were all about. The NDP didn't." In retelling this story, Sass comments, "In other words he was saying that the Conservatives understood that this was really an infringement on that fortress of management pre-rogatives. And that has never been an issue again. The Tories got rid of it, and when the NDP got into power again, was a dead issue." One of Sass's more bitter memories of this period is of the 1983 federal New Democratic Party convention, which was held in Saskatchewan to honour the fiftieth anniversary of the Regina Manifesto. A group of left-wing delegates had put forward their own manifesto. In speaking against it, Allan Blakeney took issue with a proposal for industrial democracy. According to Sass, Blakeney told the delegates that this had been tried in Saskatchewan and failed, and if they wanted to know more about why it could not work all they had to do was ask Bob Sass. If anyone had asked, Sass would have told them that industrial democracy had never been given a fair shake in Saskatchewan.

7

THE WORLD DOES NOT WORK THIS WAY

IN THE SUMMER OF 2000, just as this manuscript was reaching completion, I attended a workshop called "New Life for Tired Safety Committees." It was led by Stuart Davies, the management co-chair of the joint health-and-safety committee at New Flyer Industries, a Winnipeg-based bus manufacturing company that is also one of the more dangerous workplaces in Manitoba. From the title of the workshop it appeared that I was not alone in thinking that the committee structure was in some sort of crisis. And in an eerie way, the opening of Davies's talk mirrored many of the arguments made in this book. He said that from his experience at New Flyer and his discussions with management joint health-and-safety committee members at other workplaces, joint committees had few achievements, provided their members with very little in the way of a personal reward, and were not well connected with the larger organization.

He quickly identified two of the arguments that trade unionists have long made: the lack of a committee decision-making process and the fact that the committees are purely consultative. Davies pointed out that once a safety issue gets onto the committee agenda it is supposed to stay there until it is resolved. However, the legislation provides little guidance as to how issues are to be resolved if there are differing points of view. Items can simply re-appear on the agenda forever: hence the eternal responsibility system. And, Davies noted, even when decisions are reached, there is no guarantee that they will be acted upon. After all, he said, the safety committee still has to convince other managers that its concerns are of greater concern than the other production-related issues that they are struggling with. The committee's ability to do this depended on its credibility and resources—and currently he said he did not think most committees had very much credibility. As he quite succinctly put the issue, "the committee lacks the authority and responsibility to achieve its mandate."

The solution that Davies proposed was not to provide the committees with the authority that they need—for example, to get management to commit, at a minimum, to acting on the committee's recommendations. Instead, he proposed reducing the scope of the committee's mandate: in effect turning the health and safety committee into an employee training committee. In fact, the most telling aspect of his presentation was the fact that, even in his printed handouts, the committees were always referred to as safety committees, rather than health and safety committees. Davies suggested that committee members lack the experience and training necessary to deal with their admittedly broad mandate. His approach was to have the committee take on a role that it could accomplish given its resources and skill levels. That, he thought, would provide the committee with a sense of accomplishment and improve its credibility with management.

With a few twists and embellishments, what he was recommending was a return to the type of industrial safety programs that were introduced in the 1920s. Those campaigns all focused on reducing injuries by changing worker behaviour. There were contests for divisions that had the lowest accident rates, there were cartoon posters that featured careless workers with such condescending names as Otto Nobetter and Willie Everlearn. At New Flyer, Davies convinced the committee to buy into an accident reduction campaign that involved posters, payroll stuffers, and workplace-safety talks that usually lasted for ten minutes. While workers gave these talks, they used a pre-set text that came off of a CD. It was all very reminiscent of the health and safety talks at CN that had so bothered Bill

Quinn. Stickers, t-shirts and badges were used to provide committee members with a sense of identity and recognition. There was even a logo contest. Davies had to acknowledge that while there was much more activity and that "the committee is in charge of its own agenda," the union had been a reluctant participant in this new approach. Furthermore, the company had yet to see a drop in its accident rate.

One hundred years ago workers, not work organization, were seen as the main cause of all on-the-job injuries. And just as was the case one hundred years ago, there is now little interest in addressing health as opposed to safety issues. One of the few differences now is that workers, as members of workplace health and safety committees, are being recruited to reinforce these unfortunate messages. When this happens health and safety committees have not been revived—they have been captured. Indeed, in many instances when worker-members on committees give the committee a positive assessment, they are usually referring to the committee's ability to deal with the safety issues that are referred to it. Underlying issues never make it to the agenda. On this point, recall meatpacker Gerry Adolphe's comment that the committee in his workplace was working well but it could not even begin address the plant's major health problem: line speed.

So while the committees often do very good work, particularly in workplaces where management is prepared to cooperate, workers have not experienced these committees as a form of empowerment. And in some cases, companies have been able to use the committees as the basis for reorganizations that advance corporate quality of working life programs or simply to use them to blame the workers for any accidents that take place. In too many cases it has simply been another form of control, but perhaps the most pernicious form of control, since it gives the illusion that it is in the workers' power to look after health and safety. Failure to do so is then a failure on the part of the workers.

Davies said that his goal was to provide the committee members with some fun, to move them away from the "dark side" and their focus on pain. But the pain remains. And while ther is nothing wrong with fun, change of a far more fundamental order is required. It was in search of a list of such reforms that I travelled to Saskatoon in the fall of 1998 to meet with Bob Sass, the man whose craggy features and New York accent helped launched the health and safety movement twenty-five years ago.

I Am No Longer a Proponent of the Three Rights

SINCE HE WAS FIRED BY the Conservative government of Grant Devine nearly two decades ago, Bob Sass has taught industrial relations at the University of Saskatchewan. When the New Democratic Party was returned to power in Saskatchewan Sass was told that times had changed and there would be no support for the sort of expansion of health and safety committee powers that he has envisioned when he created the Work Environment Board. He has taken this opportunity to rethink his approach to occupational health and safety. I spent several days with Sass talking with him about his new ideas. At times there would be flashes of the Bob Sass who spread the hot gospel of the three rights. In fact, I was once more converted in his living room as he outlined the reasoning behind the reforms of the 1970s. But then his brow furrows under his curly mass of greying hair, his voice drops dramatically and he lets slip his bombshell.

> I am no more a proponent of the three rights. For the last five or six years I have been writing steadily that rights equal noise. Sass has rights, Rockefeller has rights—what does that mean? Workers have rights, management has rights, shareholders have rights, industrial hygienists have rights, consumers have rights. Yet it is worker health and safety that we are talking about. Rights do not necessarily mean dignity, self-respect, and self-esteem. For that you have to have some control regarding the future when it comes to your own health and safety. This is not the way workers across Canada experience the three rights.

For some these conclusions have the ring of heresy. Indeed, when Bob Sass says it is time to rethink the three Rs, it is a little like the Pope saying he's got serious doubts about the Trinity. Others wonder if Sass is not throwing out the baby with the bath water, turning his back on a useful reform because it failed to live up to expectations. He knows that he generates this reaction, and regrets it. Many activists, he says, "want the old Sass back. But he's gone, I have not kidnapped him." Sass does, however, qualify his comment that rights equal noise by stating that he does not want to undermine the current committees.

> We have excellent committees and activists across this country, certainly in the province of Saskatchewan, with which I am most familiar. These day-to-day activities have to go on, there is no doubt about it. And they have to get better. There is not doubt about that. On the other hand, I think we have to stop, reflect, and, after twenty-five years of occupational health and safety statute and regulations in this province, ask just what is going on?

The short answer is that, far more than most people would care to admit, the real workplace health and safety decisions are made on the basis of how much safety we can afford. Workers' health is still for sale. The workplace is not governed by either the committees or the inspectors, or in some senses even by the employer. Meatpackers do not slow down the assembly line because they want to keep their jobs. Autoworkers negotiate improvements in exposure limits, quite literally paying for improved health protection, telephone operators accept computer-driven work practises for fear of losing their jobs completely. Inspectors know, often without being told, that they have to be reasonable, meaning that they should not infringe on a company's profitability. And workplace health and safety committee members are well aware of the fact that no one will treat them like heroes if their proposals lead to job losses or a plant shutdown.

So if Bob Sass is no longer a proponent of the three Rs, just what is he proposing? First of all, he is determined not to become the author of a new legislative program for which labour can lobby. He has no interest in reprising his term as labour's health and safety guru. His recent writings on health and safety are as likely to quote poetry and philosophy as some public policy expert. And as his comments on rights-as-noise suggest, his words often seem as ambiguous as modern poetry. As I interviewed him on just this point I began to feel uncomfortable. Indeed it was almost as if I was trying to pin him down. I realized that I wanted a program. And as my questions became more leaden and persistent, his answers seemed more artful.

> Workers have to say no to things that will do harm to their well being at work. This "no" does not have to be tied to certain conditions or pre-conditions, knowledge of the Act or the regulation or the code. But it should come from their bodies. The embodiment
> ✕ will tell them if it hurts. If there is a nausea, dizziness, menstrual problems and so on. And if in the committee or the community of workers these issues matter to workers, then they have to say no to bad things—without pre-conditions or any pre-understanding as determined by some standards or principles. And then work from there.

The three ideas in that statement are central to Sass's thinking. The first is that there must be what Sass calls "an unprecedented action." It is Sass's version of Nancy Reagan's famous advice to young people to just say no to drugs. Workers, he says, must say no to hazardous conditions. And in doing this, he says workers may have to ignore the rules by which they are currently forced to play. At first blush this sounds both dangerous and highly romantic. Workers who step outside the rules, who refuse to follow an employer's direction, place themselves at tremendous risk of being disciplined and even dismissed unless they can demonstrate that they are exercising their legal, and rather limited, right to refuse. But as we talk I realize he is not talking about individual action, but coordinated actions. Later that night, between bites of Vietnamese food, Sass comments, almost in an aside, that this is what workers have always done. When you look at the history of workplace health and safety, you discover that changes have come because workers said no. The miners at Elliot Lake, the aircraft workers at McDonnell Douglas, the Manitoba telephone operators—their victories did not come from legislation, but from action. In some cases the workers were protected by the right to refuse, in other cases they weren't. But in every case, the workers I spoke with were adamant about one point. By the time they decided to refuse to do work that they thought was unsafe, they did not care what the law said—they were not working.

This ties into the second point—one that makes Sass sound somewhat like a French philosopher (and perhaps more strangely, makes French philosophers sound sensible). It has to do with language and knowledge. Despite creation of workplace health and safety committees and the right to know, worker knowledge is still devalued. Stuart Davies, for example, spoke of the fact that workers lack the knowledge to deal with many workplace health and safety issues. Indeed he said he sought to bring them up to management's level. In his revived committee, workers' experience is not seen as a form of knowledge.

Too many reforms, including Sass's own, have been based on theory. "Theory is a Greek word that relates to something that is outside of time and space, some universal quality." Sass stops for a moment, and then continues with a mournful acknowledgement, "But we are all in some space, experiencing time. The abstraction of theory lops off the worker's experience; it separates facts from values." Saying no, acting on the basis of experience, is a way of repairing this division.

Repairing the division will also involve struggle over the language of health and safety. Colin Lambert of CUPE points out that the battle over language is ongoing. "Employers no longer violate an occupational health and safety act, they are simply in a state of non-compliance. One of the most telling changes is that the federal government has removed the word enforcement from it vocabulary. We have been told by trainers who train the inspectors and train others, they no longer use 'the E-word.'" Instead of enforcing the law, the inspectors attempt to bring the employers into voluntary compliance.

In some of his work Sass takes this concern much deeper. He says that the very acts, standards and regulations that were meant to protect workers have limited the types of conversations that workers can have about health and safety. The discussion is no longer about what workers are experiencing and what they believe is happening to their health. Instead the discussion is about standards, about what is and is not acceptable. It is rules-based and individualistic.

It limits the involvement of the workplace participants to those who are knowledgeable about the act and the regulations, who can interpret the literature and so on. The act and the regulations become a technology that produces a certain behaviour. Even when it is applied, it is applied by those who are most powerful and this is why employers generally come out on top in those kinds of discussions.

In response to this individualist way of understanding, labour must draw on its communitarian traditions. Sass argues that workers' knowledge is at its heart communal knowledge. As in the case of George Smith, it arose when workers spoke to one another about their workplace experiences.

> We learn about our work environment because we have conversations. Many conversations, many discussions, many eyes, many ears, many mistakes, many this, many that, gives us awareness of what we are talking about in the work environment.

In the end Sass believes workers must say no to the pathology of a market that places their health up for auction. To do this, to assert the value of their own knowledge, workers will need to draw upon the strengths of the labour movement and its traditions. He defines these as traditions of community, solidarity and defiance. It is a movement that has always been at odds with a market-based approach to life. He both likens and links a revived health and safety movement to the feminist movement. "We must tell our stories, we must understand what was done to workers." And he says, when workers come together in this fashion and say no, not on the basis of their research or legislation but on the basis of their experiences and knowledge, because of who they are, they will be exercising power against the violence they experience in the workplace. There is no guarantee that they will win, but without action, there is a certainty of defeat.

Conclusions

THIS IS A JOURNALIST'S BOOK. It is based on many conversations and some reading. To the degree that it contributes to the sort of project Bob Sass speaks of, it attempts to remember and retell some of labour's stories. It is not a book that recounts great victories, but in some cases it is a sort of victory to make sure that defeats and tragedies are not forgotten. This is also a book that seeks to make an argument—namely that the reforms of the 1970s failed because they did not rebalance power relations in the workplace and that this failure was coupled with a de-emphasis on health and safety law enforcement because the committees were supposedly dealing with this issue.

I once planned to end this book by highlighting the need to make three obvious reforms. First, workers should constitute a majority on health and safety committees; second, that the recommendations made by such committee have the same force in law as an inspector's work order; and finally that workers have the right to strike over health and safety issues. These measures would turn what are weak rights into strong rights. Such changes are eminently justifiable—the people who put the most at risk in the productive process ought to have the greatest say over how that process goes forward. Those who risk their health and often their lives are obviously risking far more than those who have simply invested a portion of their wealth. At the same time, labour departments must develop a culture of enforcement, and be given the resources and powers to ensure that employers obey the laws.

Employers would fight these reforms tooth and nail. For very good reason—they threaten to turn the world of management rights upside down. It might be argued that such recommendations are completely out of touch with the new economy, with its emphasis on flexible workforces and global competitiveness. It could be objected there is no way that social democratic governments, entranced by the so-called Third Way (a term that means whatever they want it to mean) and its dreams of partnering and cooperating their way to a more humane capitalism, would entertain these ideas for a moment. It is old thinking, and therefore not to be contemplated. Finally, it might even be argued that workers are not demanding democracy.

Perhaps. But I still think these are good ideas. They would be worthwhile reforms. And even if they failed to make the workplace more democratic, they would "fail better" than the current regime does. Rather than single out a clutch of reforms, however, I would prefer that this book end by broadening the discussion and stressing the need and importance of bringing politics back into the debate over health and safety. Critics are right when they say that a true democratization of the workplace is incompatible with our current political system. It would also appear to have been the case that such a democratization was not possible in the so-called socialist states that existed in Eastern Europe in the twentieth century. Real change requires moving beyond our current political order. Leading voices on the left and right tell us that such change is not possible. History has rendered its judgment, and for the foreseeable future the world shall be shaped by capitalism, and we must make our peace with it.

But all history tells us with certainty is that there is change over time. And that while very few organizations ever fully achieve their goals, disaster awaits those who have no goals and no movement. Politicizing the health and safety movement means emphasizing the fact that there is no necessary link between the interests of workers and employers in this area. It means recognizing that conflict is unavoidable: it is built into the structure of our economic system. Workers will not simply say no to dangerous situations because they recognize that they are dangerous—they are trapped by the threat of unemployment, trapped by the need to provide for themselves and their families. This reality was underscored by the testimony of survivors of the Westray mine disaster, who had been told that they would not be eligible for unemployment insurance if they quit a workplace that they believed to be not only dangerous but lethal. The current political and economic order demands that workers put their health up for sale.

Efforts to politicize the health and safety movement would do more than simply increase the demands for strong rights in the workplace. They would help to create a political atmosphere for change. Those who say that capitalism has carried the day argue that it represents the best of all possible worlds because it provides people with freedom and an ever-improving standard of living. It is good for both the mind and the body. But as I write this in the summer of 2000 the financial pages are full of anxiety because the unemployment rate is getting too low. If it drops any lower workers will actually be able to exercise some real choice about where they work (choice about what goes on at those workplaces is still largely off the radar screen). And according to received wisdom, that cannot be allowed to happen. Unemployment must never reach the point where workers can ask for more money or better working conditions, secure in the knowledge that they cannot be replaced. Central bankers and investors are taking measures to cool off the economy, at the same time dousing workers' hopes of a pay raise or the opportunity to tell a bullying employer what to do with their job. The freedom to choose whether or not to risk one's life, then, is largely fictitious. And the thousands of Canadian workers who are injured on the job each year have good reason to wonder if this system really does deliver the goods in the material world.[1] Politicizing health and safety raises questions that undermine the legitimacy of our current economic system.

A movement towards expanding worker rights in the workplace may even prove to be the best way to build a political movement for a more democratically controlled economy. The Nova Scotia coal miners of the early twentieth century worked under very dangerous conditions and sought at every turn to exercise as much control as they could over their workplace. In this they drew on what was even by then a long tradition among coal miners of controlling their workplaces: a tradition so ingrained among Cornish miners that they simply refused to work in the presence of a supervisor. They had fought for and won the right to have their own inspectors, their own weighmen and a pit committee to inspect accidents and deal with grievances. They often staged brief strikes to protest the disciplining or transferring of a worker, to ensure that there were enough men to do the work safely, and to oppose the introduction of dangerous or ineffective equipment. In some cases, they would strike on the job, slowing down their production to protest pay cuts. During this period the miners conducted a number of heroic and ultimately tragic battles in defense of their jobs and their living standards. It led them to demand the "democratic organization and management of industry by the workers." Their union leader, J.B. McLachlan, claimed that the workers had already paid for the mines. "The workers have put too much into these mines. Three lives in every thousand. That is more than all the millions [the mine operators] have put in. Over a period of years they have put the money in, the workers have put their blood in." When they were run by corporations the mines were dangerous, subject to rapid busts and booms, and in the opinion of many workers wasteful. When one miner was asked by a company representative at a government commission if he really believed the miners could do a better job of running the mines he answered, "I believe it is the workmen that is running it now. I notice any time the workmen stops the mine stops." In times of crisis the miners' traditional control of their working environment was transformed to a much more radical demand: the control of the industry itself.[2]

The best retort to those who would argue that it pointless to even talk about a democratically controlled economy or a democratic workplace because the world does not work that way (and many will make those arguments) may be found in the poetry of Tom Wayman. In his poem "Paper, Scissors, Stone," he muses over the inequalities of wages of those who work with the elements of the child's game of paper, scissors and stones. We are all far more equal in our worth than our disparate paycheques might suggest. "And," he concludes:

> If anyone mentions
> this is a nice idea but isn't possible,
> consider what we have now;
> everybody dissatisfied, continually grumbling and disputing.
> No, I'm afraid it's the system that doesn't function
> except it goes on
> and will
> until we set to work to stop it
>
> with paper, with scissors, with stone.[3]

NOTES

Chapter 1:

[1] *Manitoba Reports*, Volume 5, 1889, *Rajotte v. Canadian Pacific Railway.* pp. 365–381.

[2] *Manitoba Reports*, Volume 18, 1908, *Street v. Canadian Pacific Railway.*

[3] From George Underhill, Moline, Manitoba, to Edward Brown, Provincial Treasuer, January 30, 1916.

[4] The *Voice*, July 20, 1906.

[5] *The Report of the Commission into the Workmen's Compensation Act.* Queen's Printer, Winnipeg 1958, p. 18.

[6] See also the *Labour Gazette*, June 1913, p. 1444; *Pettit v. Canadian Northern Railway*, where an award was reduced from $5,000 to $3,000.

[7] *Manitoba Reports*, Volume 19, 1909, *MacIntyre v Holiday, Manitoba Court of Appeal*, pp. 538–539.

[8] *The Labour Gazette*, June 1915, p. 1455.

[9] *Manitoba Reports*, Volume 13, 1900, *Regina v. Great West Laundry Company.* pp. 66–74.

[10] Ibid.

[11] The *Voice*, June 6, 1902.

[12] The *Voice*, September 17, 1909.

[13] The *Voice*, April 8, 1910.

Chapter 2

[1] Wallace Clement. *Hardrock Mining: Industrial Relations and Technological Changes at Inco.* McClelland and Stewart, Toronto 1981, pp. 219–250.

[2] Dan Berman. *Death On the Job.* Monthly Review Press, pp. 31-32.

[3] Harry Glasbeek and Susan Rowland. "Are Injuring and Killing at Work Crimes?" *Osgoode Hall Law Journal*, volume 17, number 3, p. 521.

[4] Charles Noble. "Regulating Work in a Capitalist Society," in *Corporate Crime: Contemporary Debate.* Frank Pearce and Laureen Snider, eds. University of Toronto, Toronto 1995.

[5] Ontario. *Report of the Royal Commission on the Health and Safety of Wokers in Mines.* (Chair J.M. Ham). Ministy of the Attorney-General, Toronto 1976. p. 121.

Chapter 3

[1] Bruce Livesey. "Profits Before People." *Business Journal*, April 1988.

2 New Strategies Sub-Committee. *Final Report.* Canadian Labour Congress, 1996.

[3] Human Resources Development Canada (Labour Branch, Occupational Safety and Health and Fire Prevention Division). *Occupational Injuries and Their Cost in Canada, 1993–1997.* Canada 1999.

[4] Stephen Brickey and Karen Grant. *An empircal study of work-related accidents and illnesses in Winnipeg.* April 1992.

[5] Allen Kraut."Estimates of the extent of morbidity and mortality due to occupatonal diseases in Canada." *American Journal of Industrial Medicine* 25 (1994). pp. 267–278.

[6] Marc Renaud and Chantal St-Jacques. "The Right to Refuse in Quebec: Five-year evolution of a new mode of expressing risk," *International Journal of Health Services*, volume 18, number 3, 1988.

[7] Eric Tucker, "The Persistence of Market Regulation of Occupational Health and Safety," in *Essays in Labour Relations Law: Papers presented at the Conference on Government and Labour Relations: the death of voluntarism.* Geoff England, ed. CCH Canadian, Don Mills 1986.

[8] Manitoba. *Annual Reports*, Department of Labour, 1995–96, 1998–99.

[9] Vivienne Walters, Wayne Lewchuk, R. Jack Richardson, Lea Anne Moran, Ted Haines, and Dave Verma. "Judgements of Legitimacy Regarding Occupational Health and Safety," in *Corporate Crime: Contemporary debate*. Frank Pearce and Laureen Snider, eds. University of Toronto, Toronto 1995, p. 290.

[10] Ibid. p. 292.

[11] Ibid, p. 295.

[12] The *Voice*, July 17, 1908.

[13] The *Voice*, September 17, 1909.

[14] W.G. Carson. "The Conventionalization of Early Factory Crime." *International Journal for the Sociology of Law*, 1979, number 7, pp. 37–60.

[15] Richard Fidler, "The Occupational Health and Safety Act and the Internal Responsibility System." *Osgoode Hall Law Journal*, volume 24, number 2, 1987. p. 335.

[16] Ibid.

[17] Ibid, p. 336.

[18] Vivienne Walters, "Company Doctors' Perceptions of and Responses to Conflicting Pressures from Labor and Management." *Social Problems*, volume 30, number 1, October 1982, p. 8.

[19] Bruce Livesey. "Profits Before People." *Business Journal*, April 1988. Wayne Roberts and George Ehring, *Giving Away a Miracle*, Oakville, Mosaic, 1993, pages 238-240.

[20] Joel Novek. "The Labour Process and Workplace Injuries in the Canadian Meat Packing Industry," *Canadian Review of Sociology and Anthropology*, volume 19, number 1 1992. p. 26.

[21] Ibid. p. 32.

[22] Tom Wayman, "Defective Parts of Speech: Official Errata," in *In a Small House on the Outskirts of Heaven*. Vancouver, Harbour, 1989. p. 58.

Chapter 4

[1] Duart Snow. "The Holmes Foundry Strike of March, 1937: 'We'll give their jobs to white men.'" *Ontario History*, volume 69, p. 1077.

2 Cited in Jim Brophy, *Review of the Ministry of Labour Documents, Caposite & Holmes Insulation Sarnia, Ontario 1958-1991.* Canadian Auto Workers 1998. p. 2.

3 Ibid, p. 19.

4 Ibid, p. 22.

5 Ibid, p. 11.

[6] Ibid, p. 21.

[7] W. McGill and F. Carlson to W. Fox-Decent, November 22, 1982 (PAM P3010, F-13-18).

[8] Mark Aldrich. *Safety First: Technology, Labour and Business in the Building of American Work Safety 1870-1939.* Johns Hopkins University, Baltimore.

[9] Manitoba Department of Labour. *Annual Report, 1994-95.* p. 55.

[10] Marc Renaud and Chantal St-Jacques. "The right to refuse in Québec: Five-year evolution of a new mode of expressing risk." *International Journal of Health Services,* bolume 18, number 3, 1988.

[11] Vivienne Walters. "State Mediation of Conflicts over Work Refusals: The Role of the Ontario Labour Relations Board." *International Journal of Health Services,* volume 21, no 4, 1991.

[12] Vivienne Walters and Ted Haines. "Workers' Use and Knowledge of the Internal Responsibility System: Limits to Participation in Occupational Health and Safety." *Canada Public Policy,* volume XIV, number 4, 1988.

[13] Eric Tucker. "The Persistence of Market Regulation of Occupational Health and Safety," in *Essays in labour relations law: papers presented at the Conference on Government and Labour Relations: the death of voluntarism.* Geoff England, ed. CCH Canadian Don Mills 1986. p. 235.

[14] Eric Tucker. "And Defeat Goes On: An Assessment of Third-Wave Health and Safety Regulation," in *Corporate Crime: Contemporary debate.* Frank Pearce and Laureen Snider, eds. University of Toronto, Toronto 1995. p. 259.

Chapter 5

[1] W.G. Carson. "The Conventionalization of Early Factory Crime." *International Journal for the Sociology of Law,* 1979, 7, p. 42.

[2] Ibid.

[3] Cathy Walker. *Submission to Workers' Compensation Board of Manitoba, Reassessment Setting Model.* May 24, 2000, Canadian Autoworkers.

[4] Eric Tucker. *Administering Danger in the Workplace: The Law and Politics of Occupational Health and Safety Regulation in Ontario, 1850-1914.* University of Toronto, Toronto 1990, p. 170.

[5] Ibid, p.169.

[6] S.A. Roach, DSc, PhD, and S. M. Rappaport, PhD. "But They Are Not Thresholds: A critical analysis of the documentation of Threshold Limit Values." *American Journal of Industrial Medicine* volume 17, 1990. p. 730.

[7] Ibid. p. 732.

[8] Ibid. p. 740.

[9] H.P. Blejer, (June 5, 1980), Letter to Colonel. V. L. Carter (Chairman, TLV Committee) cited in Barry I. Castleman, ScD and Grace E. Ziem, MD DrPH, "Corporate Influence on Threshold Limit Values." *American Journal of Industrial Medicine,* number 13 (1988) p. 553.

10 Grace E. Ziem MD, Dr PH and Barry I. Castleman, ScD. "Threshold Limit Values: Historical Perspectives and Current Practice." *Journal of Occupational Medicine,*

volume 31, number 11, November 1989, p. 913.

[11] Barry I. Castleman, ScD and Grace E. Ziem, MD DrPH. "Corporate Influence on Threshold Limit Values." *American Journal of Industrial Medicine*, number 13 (1988). pp. 531-559.

[12] Eric Tucker. "The Persistence of Market Regulation of Occupational Health and Safety." *Essays in Labour Relations Law: Papers presented at the Conference on Government and Labour Relations: the death of voluntarism.* Geoff England, ed. CCH Canadian, Don Mills 1986. p. 237.

[13] John Braithwaite. *"To Punish or Persuade: Enforcement of Coal Mine Safety.* State University of New York, Albany 1985. pp. IX-19.

[14] Ibid. pp IX-54.

[15] Government of Manitoba Department of Labour. *Annual Report*, 1951.

[16] Cited in Ministry of Labour Employee Relations Committee. *A New Lease On Life: Necessary reforms to Ontario's health and safety enforcement system, a submission to the Minister of Labour.* 1995, p. 7.

[17] Government of Manitoba Department of Labour. *Annual Report.* 1998–99.

[18] Harry Glasbeek and Susan Rowland. "Are injuring and killing at work crimes?" *Osgoode Hall Law Journal*, volume 17, number 3.

[19] Eric Tucker, "The Westray Mine Disaster and its Aftermath: The Politics of Causation." *The Canadian Journal of Law and Society*, number 10 (1995). p. 91.

Chapter 6

[1] Annalee Yassi, John L. Weeks, Kathleen Samson, Monte Raber. "Epidemic of 'Shocks' in Telephone Operators: Lessons for the medical community." *Canadian Medical Association Journal*, volume 140, April 1989, p. 820.

[2] Robert Karasek and Töres Theorell. *Healthy Work: Stress Productivity and the Reproduction of Working Life.* Basic Books, New York 1990. p. 9.

[3] Robert Kanigel. *The One Best Way: Frederick Winslow Taylor and the Enigma of Efficiency.* Viking, New York 1998. p. 11.

[4] Ibid. p. 217.

[5] Ibid. p. 377.

[6] Ibid. p. 169.

[7] Ibid. pp. 321-331. See also Harry Braverman. *Labor and Monopoly Capital: The Degradation of Work in the Twentieth Century.* Monthly Review Press, New York 1975. pp. 102-106.

[8] Robert Kanigel. *The One Best Way: Frederick Winslow Taylor and the Enigma of Efficiency.* Viking, New York 1998. p. 14.

[9] Robert Karasek and Töres Theorell. *Healthy Work: Stress Productivity and the Reproduction of Working Life.* Basic Books, New York 1990. p. 24.

[10] Robert Kanigel. *The One Best Way: Frederick Winslow Taylor and the Enigma of Efficiency.* Viking, New York 1998. p. 444.

[11] Ibid. p. 533.

[12] Robert Karasek and Töres Theorell. *Healthy Work: Stress Productivity and the Re-

production of Working Life. Basic Books, New York 1990. p. 111.

[13] From notes taken by George Bryce. *Changing Power Relationships in the Workplace, Working Paper No. 82-83*. University of Ottawa, Ottawa, p. 40–41. Cited in Robert Sass. "The Work Environment Board and the Limits of Social Democracy in Social Policy and Social Justice," in *Social Justice and Social Policy: the Blakeney Years in Saskatchewan*. Jim Harding, ed. Wilfrid Laurier University Press, 1994, p. 59.

[14] Bob Sass to the President of the Potash Corporation of Saskatchewan, December 10, 1981. Cited in Robert Sass. "The Work Environment Board and the Limits of Social Democracy in Social Policy and Social Justice," in *Social Justice and Social Policy: the Blakeney Years in Saskatchewan*. Jim Harding, ed. Wilfrid Laurier University Press, 1994, p. 72.

Chapter 7

[1] Eric Tucker, "Worker Health and Safety Struggles: Democratic Possibilities and Constraints." *New Solutions*, Winter 1996.

[2] Based on David Frank's "Contested Terrain: Workers Control in the Cape Breton Coal Mines in the 1920s," in *On the Job: Confronting the Labour Process in Canada*. Craig Heron and Robert Storey, eds. McGill-Queen's, Kingston-Montreal 1986; and Alan Derickson. *Workers' Health, Workers' Democracy: The Western Miners' Struggle, 1891-1925*. Cornell University Press, Ithaca and New York.

[3] Tom Wayman. "Paper, Scissors, Stone," in *Paperwork: An anthology*. Tom Wayman, ed. Harbour, Madeira Park, BC 1991.